TALES FROM THE

VILLANOVA WILDCATS

LOCKER ROOM

TALES FROM THE
VILLANOVA WILDCATS
LOCKER ROOM

A COLLECTION OF THE GREATEST
WILDCAT STORIES EVER TOLD

ED PINCKNEY
WITH BOB GORDON

SPORTS
PUBLISHING

Sports Publishing books may be purchased in bulk at special discounts for sales promotion, corporate gifts, fund-raising, or educational purposes. Special editions can also be created to specifications. For details, contact the Special Sales Department, Sports Publishing, 307 West 36th Street, 11th Floor, New York, NY 10018 or sportspubbooks@skyhorsepublishing.com.

Sports Publishing® is a registered trademark of Skyhorse Publishing, Inc.®, a Delaware corporation.

Visit our website at www.sportspubbooks.com.

10 9 8 7 6 5 4 3 2 1

Library of Congress Cataloging-in-Publication Data is available on file.

Cover design by Tom Lau
Cover photo credit AP Images

Print ISBN: 978-1-61321-718-4
Ebook ISBN: 978-1-61321-751-1

Printed in the United States of America

CONTENTS

INTRODUCTION

V for Villanova

"V" for Villanova, "V" for Victory
"B" for Blue and "W" for White
For the Blue and the White we will fight!
Fight! Fight! Fight!

Fight for Villanova, Fight for Victory
For we're out to win the fray;
Villanova leads the way,
With a capital "V" for Victory.

For we're out to beat the foe
Show the en-e-my we know
How to win with a "V" for Victory.
Vill-a-no-va V-I-L-L-A-N-O-V-A
"V" for Vic-tor-y V-I-C-T-O-R-Y

—Villanova fight song

Stop a student on the Villanova campus and ask whether his or her school is (a) an academic institution or (b) a sport factory where handsome school buildings serve as an idyllic backdrop for the real business at hand (sports) ... then sit back and wait for a quizzical stare. Most likely, your listener is a half-listener—distracted or preoccupied about an upcoming engineering, philosophy, or chemistry quiz. The answer to your question is too obvious to them. Little Villanova (yes, little— there are only 6,000-plus full-time undergraduate students dispersed around this tidy suburban campus) is a bona fide, crack-the-books-or-relinquish-your-space-to-a-real-student kind of school. Old-fashioned values rule, fueling a long-standing work-hard, play-hard tradition. The tradition nourishes a successful sport heritage. But sport is ancillary. Education is the thing in the halls of Villanova. It's just that those halls lie close to some pretty famous sporting venues. The Jake Nevin Field House, the Pavilion, and the Jumbo Jim Elliott Stadium have been the stage for some celebrated athletes and teams.

For certain, Villanova can boast a disproportionate number of puff-the-chest-out athletic feats and triumphs. But that's not what Villanova is about. That's not how Villanovans view Villanova. And that's definitely not how they go about their business.

In the words of Jim Murray, Villanova's former sports information director, former Philadelphia Eagles' general manager, and current owner of a PR firm: "You can't put the Villanova tradition into words, but you can put it into people."

In track and field, Villanova has produced more than 40 Olympians, who have won six gold medals and three silvers. As Murray observes, "That's more than some countries."

Villanova produces big-time results without the big-time look or the act. Their athletes and programs seem to excel despite an understated infrastructure. A Jim Murray story tells it all:

"*Sports Illustrated* sent over a writer to do a cover story on our track team in '68 (that year, five Villanova athletes went to Mexico City for the Olympics. One of them, Larry James, won a gold medal and set a world record in the 400 meters). This guy heard of Jumbo Jim Elliott and Villanova and figured we had a big-time operation. I walked him back to meet the guys and there was Erv Hal, Dave Patrick, and Larry James shoveling the snow off the track so they could work out. The guy said, 'They aren't even complaining.' I said, 'Welcome to Villanova.'"

Villanova University was founded in 1842, but its academic roots and tradition go deeper.

In 1794, a Roman Catholic Order, the Augustinian Fathers, arrived in North America. Father John Rossiter, O.S.A. (Order of St. Augustine) came to minister to southeastern Pennsylvania and Delaware. A couple years later, Father Matthew Carr joined Father Rossiter. Carr was a mover, albeit not a Shaker (the Shakers were a Protestant religious sect that settled in Ephrata, a bit farther west than Villanova).

Carr had his mind set on building a much-needed Catholic church in Philadelphia. At the time, the City of Brotherly Love was the New World's largest city and the second largest English-speaking city on the globe (you don't need to be a *Jeopardy* contestant to know London was the largest). Carr wasted no time taking care of business. Within a month of his arrival, he announced his plans to erect a new church. His project evoked an enthusiastic response from Catholics and Protestants alike. The Protestant contingent included President George Washington. The father of our country-elect was a Philadelphian at the time. His temporary residency in the City of Brotherly Love owed to the fact that Philly was the fledgling nation's capital for a while during his administration. Another notable name on the contributor list was Commodore John Barry, Father of the U.S. Navy-elect, and namesake to the majestic bridge that currently strides the Delaware River near the city of Chester.

By September of 1796, six months after he embarked at Philly, Carr witnessed the setting of the cornerstone for his church at 4th and Vine Streets in Old City. Yellow fever epidemics and chronic money problems delayed progress. When finally completed on June 7, 1801, the new St. Augustine's, the first church established by the Brothers of the Order of the Hermits of St. Augustine in America, was the largest church in Philadelphia. There's a good chance it had the longest name as well.

A Philadelphia architect, Nicholas Fitz Maurice Fagan, designed and built the church, which turned out to be quite an ornate structure by New World standards. The interior featured paintings by Italian Renaissance master Tintoretto as well as other works by Old World Italian artists Carracci and Perugino.

St. Augustine's can even claim a spot in the Liberty Bell saga. Everyone knows the story of the Liberty Bell. Unfortunately, most of us know the wrong story. The Liberty Bell neither rang nor cracked on July 4, 1776. It cracked long before that. The colonists ordered a replacement bell. Meanwhile they had the original bell recast and set in place (Presumably they weren't Wharton School grads—an anachronism, I know, since Wharton School wasn't born till 1881, But in 1776, the U of P already had some graduates running around the city). When the replacement bell arrived, it wasn't needed—at least not for the State House. Somehow, the new bell found a home in the bell tower at St. Augustine's.

Philadelphia's Liberty Bell

What's Philly's most prized possession, besides Donovan McNabb, Jim Thome, Ed Pinckney, and other local heroes? It's probably the Liberty Bell. The major difference between the Liberty Bell and the sport heroes is that the athletes are free to leave Philly whenever they please. The Liberty Bell cannot. Ever wonder who owns the Liberty Bell? It's the City of Philadelphia and it can't leave Philadelphia. Why? The Bell was being exhibited all over the nation around the turn of the century, and it was getting damaged in the process. Thirty pounds of metal were chipped away for souvenirs. The Bell was never a very good bell to begin with. It cracked when it was first tested and had to be recast. Then when it was tested again, too much copper was added and the tone sounded as bad as Steve Lappas singing "My Girl." (More on that later.) The Bell was recast a second time when more silver was added.

No, the Liberty Bell never rang on July 4, 1776. It rang on July 8, 1776. Exactly 59 years later, when Chief Justice Marshall died, it rang again and it cracked again. The Bell rang for the last time on Washington's Birthday in 1846 and the crack extended.

The Liberty Bell symbolizes much, and highlights an important lesson that is often overlooked: proofreading is important. Those red squiggly lines on your computer under the misspellings can prevent eternal embarrassment. Unfortunately, the makers of the Liberty Bell didn't have spell check. Next time you visit the Liberty Bell, take note that "Pennsylvania" is spelled Pensylvania on the bell. I'm looking at a red squiggly line under it right now. I hope my proofreaders miss it.

St. Augustine's

St. Augustine's became one of Philadelphia's cultural attractions, serving as the venue for such high-profile events as the Philadelphia premiere of Handel's *Messiah*. One of the Church's musical directors, Henry Gordon Thunder, who organized the Choral Society of Philadelphia, later played a role in the 1900 founding of the Philadelphia Orchestra, which grew from the group of instrumentalists who accompanied his Chorale. The Philadelphia Orchestra, of course, achieved worldwide renown, particularly under the aegis of conductors Leopold Stokowski and Eugene Ormandy.

St. Augustine's started a school for boys in 1811, which was the precursor to Villanova University. Life was a struggle for the Augustinians in their city location. Near the mid-1800s, they looked west of the city for a less pricey location. They found one on the current Main Line (how things change!). The property they hit upon was known as Belle Air—a 100-acre plot owned by the estate of John Rudolph. Rudolph, a Catholic and wealthy area merchant, had passed away in 1838. By 1841, his heirs elected to auction off the estate. Prior to the auction, two Augustinians, Father Moriarty and Father Kyle, approached the family and negotiated a sale, reportedly for $18,000 (a good chunk less than the 2014 Villanova tuition stipend). On January 5, 1842, considered nowadays as the date Villanova was founded, title to the Belle Air property was conveyed formally to the Augustinians. Father O'Dwyer was named the first president, and on St. Augustine's Day, August 28, 1843, the new monastery and college were placed under the patronage of St. Thomas of Villanova, a 16th century Spanish archbishop. Henceforth, the compound was called Villanova. Belle Air receded into history as the fledgling institution known as Villanova opened its doors to boys of high school age and younger.

What Became of St. Augustine's

The Philadelphia of the 1840s was a tumultuous place. Nativists, a radical political group, were terrorizing immigrants and Catholics, particularly Irish Catholics. The Nativists decried foreign interference in American affairs, demanding that only native-born Americans be elected to government posts. They were outraged at Bishop Kenrick's (the Bishop of Philadelphia) petition to the Philadelphia School Board. Kenrick requested that Catholic students in public schools be allowed to use the Douay-Rheims version of the Bible for their daily devotionals in class. Public schools at the time kicked off the school day with a recitation of the Lord's Prayer, readings from the King James version of the Bible, and group singing of Protestant hymns.

The Board responded favorably, which fanned the glowing embers of mistrust of Catholics into a blaze in May 1844. On May 8, the Nativists assembled at City Hall and set out for Kensington, where there was a huge concentration of Irish immigrants. Intending to torch the Hibernia Hose Company, a volunteer group chartered by Irish-American residents, the ugly mob also set St. Michael's Church aflame, along with

St. Charles Borromeo's Seminary and several area homes. After devastating Kensington, the mob slithered back toward Philly (Kensington was not yet incorporated into the city of Philadelphia). En route they encircled St. Augustine's. They ignored the pleas of city mayor Samuel Rhoads, and the militia, and set the church ablaze. The tolling of the State House bell and the clanging of fire-engine bells increased the cacophony of the mayhem.

The following morning, only a sooty wall behind the altar remained, bearing charred testimony to the grandiose edifice that had once stood there. The 3,000-volume library was reduced to ashes. The sister bell to America's Liberty Bell was smashed after tumbling from the heights of the spire to the ground.

The implications of the riots were powerful. On September 18, 1843, the brand new Villanova College had admitted its first seven students. When the riots hit the following spring, the matriculation numbers had swollen to 40-something. During the May riots, Villanova students were sent home while the faculty stood sentry over Villanova's buildings and grounds. Fortunately, the wave of destruction did not roll beyond the city limits. However, the Augustinian fathers lacked the necessary resources to reconstruct their Philadelphia property while sustaining the Villanova property. They were forced to abandon St. Augustine's in the city. St. Charles Borromeo Seminary followed a similar path. Ultimately, the seminary abandoned its city enclave and relocated to the Main Line, across the road from St. Joseph's University's current plot at the western limits of Philadelphia.

The University Today

The attractive campus that sprawls idyllically along Lancaster Pike just west of Bryn Mawr gives no hint of those troubled beginnings. Over the ensuing 160-some years, Villanova has prospered and grown. The first student body of seven in 1843 has ballooned to over 10,000, including 6,300 full-time undergraduates in 2004.

Villanova started as a Liberal Arts College, officially sanctioned to grant degrees as of March 10, 1848. In 1905, an Engineering School was added; in 1922 the College of Commerce and Finance was recognized. On November 10, 1953, Villanova College became Villanova University with the addition of a Nursing School and School of Law.

Villanova Basketball

Somehow Villanova managed to survive its first 80 years without basketball. Then on December 21, 1920, Villanova trotted its first five guys out to the hardwoods for NCAA competition. The Villanova five that day kicked off a winning tradition with a win against Catholic University at Alumni Hall at Villanova. The 'Nova starters were: Francis C. Pickett, Norman M. Jones, Charles B. Laughlin, John B. Ryan, and Sydney F. Sweeney. In a nip-and-tuck battle, Villanova battled back in the final minutes to squeak out a 43-40 victory under Coach Michael Saxe, a University of Pennsylvania alumnus.

Prior to that season, Villanova played pick-up games against YMCAs and local teams like Crescent Athletic Club. Basketball was a relatively new (and perhaps unrecognizable) sport in 1920. Organized games had been played on the Villanova campus since about 1910. The school didn't compete formally, however, because the old gym was too small. Alumni Hall, site of the first game, was known as College Hall in its early years.

Built in 1841, Alumni Hall is the oldest building on campus. In the school's early years, it was the site where most classes and other activities took place.

Villanova's First Year on the NCAA Hardwoods

Date	Opponent	Score
December 21	Catholic University	43-40 W
January 8	at Temple	31-28 W
January 15	St. Joseph's	31-22 W
January 19	at Navy	20-46 L
January 22	Lebanon Valley	42-35 W
January 26	Fordham	22-31 L
January 28	Alumni	25-19 W
January 29	at Rahway, YMCA	44-17 W
February 2	at Army	17-47 L
February 3	at Seton Hall	14-28 L
February 4	at Crescent Athletic Club	21-40 L
February 5	at Fordham	17-24 L
February 8	Temple	36-24 W
February 16	at St. Joseph's	24-14 W

The Early Days

In its maiden season, the Blue and White, as the team was nicknamed in 1920, chalked up an 8-7 record. Half the victories came against future Big Five rivals, St. Joe's and Temple. Saxe coached from 1920 through 1926, racking up a 64-30, .681 record, with nary a losing season. John Cashman replaced Saxe for the '25-'26 campaign when the team went 11-7. Cashman however remained only two more seasons. Both were losing seasons. George Jacobs took over and turned things around with an 11-6 mark for the '29-'30 season. Jacobs lasted seven seasons before the legendary Al Severance started his reign. Severance's first two squads posted 15-8 and 25-5 records. His '37-'38 squad surprised the NIT-champion Temple Owls 36-28. The following year, however, the 20-5 Wildcats became one of the first four teams ever to appear in an NCAA Final Four. The NCAA Tournament kicked off in 1939. The 'Cats, representing the Middle Atlantic States, whipped Brown, the standard bearer for the New England States. Ohio State defeated Wake Forest. All the games were played at the Palestra. Villanova squared off against Ohio State in the semifinals for the right to play the western division winner in the championship. The Buckeye 5'11" forward, Captain Jim Hull, raised the Palestra scoring mark to 28 as Ohio State blew the Wildcats out 53-36. The 'Cats earned the dubious distinction of scoring 10 points in the first half, still the all-time NCAA record. The two-team total of 35 first-half points is second lowest in the NCAA tournament record books. Ohio State went on to the finals only to lose to Oregon in the first NCAA final.

Pitchin' Paul

One day in 1947, Coach Severance attended a Philadelphia-area tournament that a bunch of his Villanova boys were participating in. Severance was merely a spectator. The guy who won the tournament MVP that day had a killer jump shot that caught the coach's eye. Severance approached the kid afterward and asked him if he would consider coming to Villanova the next year. To the Coach's surprise, the reply came back: "I'm already a student at Villanova."

Severance invited him to try out for the team, which he did, and the legend of Paul Arizin was off and running. No book on Villanova basketball can fail to mention Paul Arizin.

Arizin didn't bother trying out for the Villanova basketball team because he never played high school ball. He was cut twice at LaSalle High.

Arizin's forte was his jump shot. According to lore, Arizin perfected it while he was at St. Monica's in South Philly. Arizin has always maintained: "I was a pretty good one-handed shooter. When I tried shooting on the slippery floors at St. Monica's, I would slip. I was also a pretty good jumper, and I found that by leaving my feet when I shot, I could avoid slipping. The more I did it, the better I got, and eventually, practically all my shots were jump shots."

Arizin was a pioneer, a founding father of the jump shot in a game that had been dominated for three-quarters of a century by the set shot. On the power of his jumper, Villanova's most famous walk-on not only made the team, but by the time his college career was over, he had become Villanova's first 1,000-point scorer, first consensus All-American, and holder of the school's single-game scoring record. Arizin's 85 points against the Naval Air Material Center tops the Villanova list to this day.

In 1950, Arizin won the collegiate national scoring title, averaging 25.3 ppg and tossing in 735 points, just five shy of the then-NCAA record. He made the Associated Press, United Press, *Sporting News*, Helms Foundation, and Catholic first-team All-America teams. He was also honored as the Helms Foundation and *Sporting News* Player of the Year.

Arizin moved on to a Hall of Fame professional career. He starred for the Philadelphia Warriors, teaming with legends like Wilt Chamberlain, Guy Rodgers, and Tom Gola (Philadelphians all). In his heyday, the Warriors were the Boston Celtics' biggest rival. Coming into the NBA with the likes of Boston's Bob Cousy and Bill Sharman, Arizin immediately attained marquee status. He finished his rookie season sixth in scoring. The following year, he dethroned the legendary George Mikan as NBA scoring champ and copped the NBA All-Star game MVP. Arizin anchored the world-champion

Philadelphia Warriors in 1956. Four times he finished first or second among NBA scorers, and in 1971, he was selected for the NBA Silver Anniversary Team.

35 Wildcats in the NBA

Paul Arizin led 'Nova's NBA parade. Arthur Spector, '41, was first, playing for the Celtics from '46-'50. Herman "Red" Klotz, '44, played for Baltimore in '47-'48. Arizin's teammate Sherwin Raiken, also in the Class of 1950, played briefly with the New York Knicks.

After Arizin's graduation, Wildcat basketball continued to purr. Larry Hennessey, (number nine on the all-time Villanova scoring list, right ahead of Arizin) and James Mooney (number six on the all-time Villanova rebounding list) led the 'Cats to successive 25-7, 19-8, and 19-8 seasons. Hennessy toiled in the NBA a few seasons with Philadelphia. His mate Mooney also logged a few NBA miles with Baltimore and Philadelphia.

In 1954, Bob Schaefer earned All-America honors. The "Blonde Bomber" as he was tagged, was the first Wildcat to surpass 2,000 points. He still ranks third on the school's all-time scoring list.

Coach Severance retired in 1961 with a glittery 413-201, .673 record. Over the next dozen years, his replacement, Jack Kraft, went on to fashion the best won-lost record in the school's history.

Villanova zoomed into the sixties and the Jack Kraft era on the wings of two Philly-grown superstars, Hubie White out of West Philadelphia High, and Wali Jones of Overbrook.

Wali Jones starred with Walt Hazzard at Philly's Overbrook High before becoming an All-American at Villanova and an NBA star. (Photo courtesy of the Villanova Sports Information Department)

The Overbrook Five

When Overbrook High School in Philadelphia jogged into Penn's Palestra in 1958 and won the city basketball title for the second straight year, the starting five included sophomore guards Wali Jones and Walt Hazzard, and senior center Wayne Hightower. Overbrook was in the middle of an unprecedented 66-2, three-year run. In that stretch, they became the first basketball team in city history to string together three straight championships. In '58, Hightower was the game's top scorer, just as he had been in '57. His 23 points fell 12 shy of the existing record for points in a city-championship game set a few years earlier by Overbrook's Wilt Chamberlain. In the '58 game, Richie Richman, Overbrook's quarterback, netted 13, which was equalled by his frontcourt mate, Ralph Heyward as the 'Brook toppled Bishop Neumann, 71-54. The following year Overbrook destroyed West Catholic, 72-53. Wali's 24 points on 10-14 shooting topped all scorers as Hazzard chipped in 16, and Heyward 20.

Hightower continued to trace Wilt's path. He went to Kansas, where he became an All-American. He was the San Francisco Warriors' 1962 first-round draft choice and enjoyed a 10-year peripatetic pro career. Hazzard became the lynchpin of John Wooden's UCLA Bruins dynasty where he achieved All-America honors in '64. In '64, Hazzard was the fifth player drafted to the NBA where he starred for 10 years, averaging as high as 24 ppg in the '67-'68 season with Seattle. Wali, of course, sizzled on the great 'Nova teams of the mid-sixties. Wali was also a '64 All-American and a pro star for 12 years.

"Wali Wonder"

Wali Jones was one of the most colorful Big Five performers ever. The press dubbed him "Wali Wonder." The Wonder was a 1964 All-American, and a 12-year pro. For several years, he'd been working for the Miami Heat—Ed Pinckney's employer for a number of years. But Wali has not been converted to a full-fledged Floridian. He still bleeds Villanova blue. The amiable legend admits that he takes advantage of every excuse to get back to Villanova or Philadelphia. He has one skeleton in the closet however—one that will make old-time Philadelphia basketball fans wince (WARNING! The following paragraph contains graphic material that is not recommended for veterans of the Wilt-Russell wars).

WALI JONES: "Do you know why I wore those black sneaks in college? I was a Celtic fan growing up. I couldn't help it! The Celtics always won, and they played a wide-open game that I loved. Don't get me wrong. I loved Philly. I always will, but I thought those Celtic black sneaks looked cool. I convinced our coach Jack Kraft to let our team wear them. I also started a fad of wearing a beret and a tan coat. Some of the older fans might remember. The other guys on the team picked up on it, and the press started calling us 'Kraft's Commandos.'"

Jones anchored a strong Villanova team that climbed as high as number six in 1964. His teammate Jim Washington was also a stellar performer, with a mini-Paul Arizin story of his own. Washington never played basketball till his senior year at Philly's West Catholic. Big Jim was drafted number one by the St. Louis Hawks and spent 10 years in the NBA. He still ranks second on the 'Cats all-time rebounding list.

Greatness

Hubie White was selected to the 1962 All-America squad. Jones earned the same honor in 1964, as did Bill Melchionni in 1966. However, the Howard Porter era was arguably Villanova's longest sustained run of greatness. Porter was Villanova's only three-time All-American. Porter-led teams posted records of 21-5, 22-7, and 23-6. In his senior year, the 'Cats clawed their way to the NCAA Finals but could not dislodge UCLA from their unprecedented seven-year reign. The 'Cats succumbed

68-62. They led briefly, 22-21, early in the game. But UCLA soon overtook them, and Villanova chased them the rest of the way. The Wildcats rallied as the game waned, twice sneaking within three, 61-58, and 63-60, but UCLA staved off each assault. The Bruins' victory over the Wildcats was their narrowest victory margin in all their championship wins.

The '71 Cats

The Wildcat starting five in 1971 was Clarence Smith, Tom Inglesby, Chris Ford, Hank Siemiontowski, and Howard Porter. Kraft had reached down into the Sunshine State to woo Porter, a high-profile star at Booker High in Sarasota Florida. Clarence Smith was a 6'8" power forward from Harrisburg, Pennsylvania. The three other starters were locals. Ford starred for Holy Spirit in Absecon, New Jersey. Siemiontowski was an All-Catholic from Philly's North Catholic High, while Inglesby was All-Catholic at Cardinal O'Hara.

The 1971 team made it to the NCAA Finals, but lost to UCLA. (Photo courtesy of the Villanova Sports Information Department)

Howard Porter (left) and Wali Jones (right) return to Philadelphia for Hall of Fame induction. (Photo courtesy of the Villanova Sports Information Department)

The talent of this squad was, if not unheralded, underheralded. Porter, of course, was a three-time All-American who moved on to a six-year NBA career with Chicago, New York, and Detroit. All his teammates also moved on to at least modest success on the hardwoods. Siemiontowski enjoyed a career in the European leagues. Clarence Smith became a Harlem Globetrotter. Tom Inglesby was Atlanta's second-round draft pick in '73. He played only briefly in the NBA. Chris Ford forged a long NBA career both as a player and coach. He followed a year with the Pistons with a nine-year stint in Boston.

His coaching career began in 1990 when he was named Celtics' skipper. He remained there until 1995. In 1998, he became head coach for Milwaukee, and from 1999-2000, he held that post for the LA Clippers. In 2003, Ford returned to Philly as the Philadelphia 76ers' new interim sheriff. As this book went to press about ten years back, Ford's battles with superstar Allen Iverson spruced up many a slow news night.

Jack Kraft was one of Villanova's greatest coaches and coached the '71 team to a near national championship. (Photo courtesy of the Villanova Sports Information Department)

Coaches

Coach Kraft's fabulous career ended on a sour note. The '72-'73 Wildcats shot off to a blistering 6-0 start, then cooled down to a dismal 11-14 record for the season. Rollie Massimino became the new mentor in 1973. The 19-year Massimino era included the Wildcats' only NCAA championship.

Rollie's teams limped off to back-to-back losing seasons—the first time in almost three decades Villanova strung losing seasons together. After that, Rollie's program kicked in. His teams would endure only two more losing campaigns. Massimino's program produced several NBA performers: Alex Bradley, Stewart Granger, Dwayne McClain, Ed Pinckney, John Pinone, Harold Pressley, Rory Sparrow, and Doug West.

Rollie's former assistant, Steve Lappas, succeeded him. Lappas spent nine years at the helm fashioning a 174-110, .613 mark. Like his predecessor, Lappas opened inauspiciously with a losing season in '92-'93. By '94-'95, he had turned things around. His Kerry Kittles-led Wildcats won the school's only Big East crown that year after trouncing Connecticut 94-78. 'Nova had played in the NIT Tournament in '93-'94, but for the next three seasons, the 'Cats were invited into the March Madness. In the Lappas era, John Celestand, Kerry Kittles, Michael Bradley, Tim Thomas, and Alvin Williams all graduated to the NBA. Coach Jay Wright is currently upholding the Wildcat tradition.

Jake Nevin

"Jake had a spiritual quality that glowed and radiated. Talking to Jake was like talking to a favorite uncle, the Irish cop on the corner,

or your parish priest. He was an earthly little saint who looked like
a leprechaun and spoke like a wise man."

          —Bill Powers, ex-Villanova basketball player

If Jake Nevin were a leprechaun, then Villanova would be his
pot o' gold and rainbow's end. Though Jake died in the house
where he was born, Villanova was unmistakenly his home. Jake
walked to Villanova every day—two and a half miles each way.
He never married. Villanova was his family. Villanova athletes
were "his kids."

    Harry Stuhldreher, one of Notre Dame's immortal Four
Horsemen, was the Wildcat football coach in 1929. That was

Jake Nevin, shown here at the end of his days at Villanova, became a leg-
end over five decades as a trainer. (Photo courtesy of the Villanova Sports
Information Department)

the year Jake Nevin arrived at Villanova—the year Wall Street laid an egg. That's the year Villanova hatched a roaster.

Jake Nevin could roast "victims" with the best of them. For more than a half-century, the leprechaun trainer brought athletes gently down to earth with his craggy, roasting cut-ups and killer one-liners. Jake's quips were never mean-spirited. His style could tumble the haughty or uplift the dispirited, as the situation dictated. He helped generations of young athletes survive and conquer crises of confidence and doubt. He helped kids embrace their limitations and laugh at their imperfections. But I'm jumping ahead.

Harry Stuhldreher needed a trainer in 1929, and 19-year-old Jake was his man. Jake took the job for life. Over the next five decades, he grew into a larger than life Villanova institution. There are more Jake tales on campus than tales about any of Villanova's other rich and famous athletes. That includes Howie Long—and that's saying something, given all the tales about Howie.

Jake was inducted into the Philadelphia Hall of Fame and the Big Five Hall of Fame in 1974. His honorary jersey, number 1, was retired at Villanova. Everyone who enters Villanova's Jake Nevin Fieldhouse is reminded of his legacy. At the dedication ceremonies for the Jake Nevin Field House, Villanova president Father Driscoll announced: "It is remarkable to note that despite a social revolution and the changing lifestyles of the young, Jake's rapport with them has never changed. The friendships of the eighties are as warm and as deep as those of the fifties ... It is truly a triumph of the human spirit."

The Women

In 1953, the all-male bastion of Villanova admitted its first class of nurses. It wasn't till 1969, however, that the women officially took to the hardwoods. The program got rolling with a scrimmages-only '68-'69 campaign. Villanova then hired Liz Cawley as a part-time coach for the first season of women's basketball ('69-'70). The team went 4-7 in its maiden season, playing their games in St. Mary's Hall, a matchbox venue. If St. Mary's was unavailable, they used whatever gym was available. Jane Sefranek (now Jane Stoltz) arrived as head coach in 1970. Jane had played in the successful Cabrini College basketball

1987 Kodak All-American Shelley Pennefather in action for the Wildcats. (Photo courtesy of the Villanova Sports Information Department)

program. She was a grad assistant at Villanova in 1970. She remained at 'Nova and grew the roundball program through 1975, compiling a 50-24 log in the process.

Since those early days, Villanova women's basketball has successively and successfully ascended to the AIWA Division II, AIWA Division I, and NCAA Division I levels, as well as joining the Big East.

Starting in 1985, the women hosted a Christmas Invitational, the Wildcat/Havoline Women's Basketball Classic. In that first tourney, Villanova legend Shelly Pennefather scored 44 and 33 points in consecutive games against Cheyney University and the University of Washington. Her exploits netted her a Tournament MVP.

In their relatively brief but shining history, the Lady 'Cats have already claimed three regular-season Big East titles ('83-'84, '84-'85, and '86-'87), and three Tournament championships ('86, '87, and 2003).

The '85 NCAA Championship

Villanova's athletic crown is studded with gems, but the crown jewel remains the miracle of 1985, when a group of nice kids-next-door shocked the entire sport world. The '85 squad's success is all the more laudable because the school succeeded wihout compromising its priorities. In this era when big money and the lure of big money threaten to corrupt athletic programs everywhere, Villanova fights to remain focused on what an institution of higher learning should.

The group of kids who won the NCAA crown in '85 managed to maintain focus in the classroom and on the court. Their leader and star was Ed Pinckney, a beloved—and adopted—Philly sport icon. Here's Ed's view of how that '85 miracle unfolded, along with reflections, anecdotes, and quips from his teammates, coaches, and other members of Rollie Massimino's Villanova "family."

But before getting into the Pinckney era at Villanova, let's trace the path that led Ed Pinckney to Villanova.

TALES FROM THE
VILLANOVA WILDCATS
LOCKER ROOM

Chapter One

ED PINCKNEY:
THE ROAD TO VILLANOVA

"Some friends give me a hard time about that photo." Ed Pinckney is smiling as he points to the cover of Villanova's 2003-2004 media guide. The cover shows the Villanova coaching staff assembled en masse at center court. Pinckney looms above the rest of the group. "I'm the only one in the picture who's not smiling. My friends said they weren't used to seeing me so serious. They were worried that I changed now that I'm a coach."

He hasn't. It's just noticeable when Ed Pinckney isn't smiling—kind of like a disturbance in the Force to his friends.

His smile and genial manner have brought him respect and love—things he cherishes more than money. After 12 years of NBA life, Ed Pinckney has emerged from the odyssey as the same down-to-earth-except-when-skying-above-the-rim guy Villanova crowds used to cheer.

Pinckney's smile is still there, same as it ever was. He articulates his smiles with shrugs and muted gestures. Everything about him is unhurried, unharried, and uncontrived—characteristics that netted him the nickname E-Z Ed.

1

Ed Pinckney is shown here during in his playing days for the Sacramento Kings. (Photo courtesy of the Villanova Sports Information Department)

"There's no one better suited to his nickname than E-Z Ed," former Pinckney teammate Dwayne McClain told me. "That name says it all. He's been E-Z Ed since the day I met him. He's never changed."

Pinckney is beloved at Villanova. "Pinckney is God" the banners read in E-Z Ed's heyday—a heresy Villanova's Augustinian fathers didn't refute or even dispute in April 1985.

Pinckney was deified on the Villanova campus of the early eighties—Pinckney the guy, not just Pinckney the basketball player. Ed Pinckney and the rest of the Wildcat basketball team were an integral part of campus life. They weren't a glamorous sideshow sequestered in chic digs away from their fellow classmen. Basketball players lived in the regular student dorms. They ate with the rest of the student body, attended classes with the rest of the students, and were campus-bound for the school year as much as their fellow students. Actually, they were more campus-bound. Few 'Nova basketball players had cars. Consequently, Villanovans got to see Ed Pinckney not only on the basketball court, but also on campus. He's the Pinckney they deified—the person, not just the rebounder, shot-blocker, and scorer.

Ultimately, his classmates loved Pinckney because there's no bombast or pretense in the guy. That's refreshing. Given enough time, most good things tend to go bad in this world. Ed Pinckney hasn't. Sure, time has advanced him a couple of decades. He's no longer the skinny kid who looked overmatched against the powerful Patrick Ewing. Pinckney's face has matured. But it remains unfurrowed by frowns. He's the poster child for the old saw about the virtues of the smile. Smiling conserves your face, keeps you young—or so the old saw goes. Frowning ages you because it requires more muscles. Being E-Z Ed has its payoffs.

Some people exude charisma in passion and intensity. Ed Pinckney does not. He simply comes across as a likeable guy, an ordinary man who accomplishes extraordinary things.

E-Z Ed seems to be that rare individual with the wisdom to stretch his horizons and not bend himself out of shape in the process. He's logged some world-class miles since his days as a schoolyard kid in the Bronx. But Ed Pinckney hasn't changed.

The Young Ed Pinckney

I was born on March 27, 1963. I grew up in in the Monroe Housing Project in the southeastern part of the Bronx. As a kid, my life centered around PS100 Park across the street from my house. I lived at that park! But I didn't play basketball all that much. I played softball and handball most of the time. It wasn't till seventh grade that I got into basketball. I wasn't playing it seriously—just for fun. I had no serious aspirations to play ball for a living.

Now This Is What I Call a Park

Ed Pinckney observes that there's an enormous difference between parks in his hometown of New York and Philadelphia.

When we talk about a park in the Bronx, we mean a break between buildings paved with concrete or that rubbery surface. When I came to Philly, I went to center city and saw the parks here. They're not what we call parks in New York! In Philly, a park means a wide-open space with trees and grass. I guess you could say that in Philly, a park is really a park.

I love New York. I love New York …

Education First

My dad never played basketball. My dad and mom were both tall, but neither one ever played basketball. My dad was a good baseball player. But he was working too hard all the time, trying to support our family. He didn't have time to play ball with me. He had to work a couple of jobs to get by. He used to get up at three or four in the morning for work and he wouldn't get back till that night. He just didn't have time for fun things. My mother was a nurse. She was busy too. My sisters and I sort of found sports on our own. We all found our way to college too, but my parents encouraged us. They thought education and college were important. So we all went to college. We were the first generation in our family who did.

Basketball Beginnings

In the summer of seventh grade, I started playing more hoops. My friend Tyrone got me into it. We called him Todd. Todd used to set up neighborhood games, our neighborhood against another one. He was a grade ahead of me and he just knew his way around. I didn't. We started to travel a little outside the neighborhood, and I got to see more of the world than ever before.

When school started that fall, Todd and I used to get up early and go to the courts across from PS 131. The freshmen in high school had the courts first. Their classes started at 8:30, ours started at 8:45. So when they left for school, we'd hop on and play up to the last possible minute. That was my routine—up at seven every day so I could get to the courts before school.

That summer, Todd took me over to Harlem to play. It was eye-popping. I went there thinking I knew how to play. Then I saw these guys doing all these amazing things! That was the first time I saw guys actively working on improving their game.

We played all day, every day all summer. We'd play a game at nine in the morning, then another at one in the afternoon someplace else, and then another at five or six. I'd hop the train after the last game each day, go home, go to bed, get up and be back playing ball at nine the next morning.

Adlai Stevenson High

I went to Adlai Stevenson High. I didn't give a thought about trying out for the team till my friend Rickey kept on telling me he could make the team and I couldn't. I didn't think I was good. But I thought I was better than Rickey. So I tried out. I still don't know why I made the team. The tryouts were just five-on-five games, nothing special. I didn't do anything special when I was on the court. But after practice, the coach came over to the benches where everyone was sitting. Rickey and I were next to each other. The coach didn't ask Rickey to come back next day. He asked me. I was shocked.

Posting Pinckney Up

Steve Post was Ed Pinckney's coach at Adlai E. Stevenson High. Ed keeps in contact with Steve to this day, crediting Coach Post as a major positive influence on his development as a person and player. Post has an unusual resumé for a successful basketball coach. He didn't play high school or college basketball. He attended Christopher Columbus High School (the school that produced Connie Hawkins) and Hunter College (now called Lehman College), both in the Bronx. While he was teaching at Park East High School, an alternative school in Manhattan, he helped coach the basketball team. When an opportunity arose to coach basketball at Stevenson, Steve seized it. He was in his sophomore year as head coach when Ed Pinckney arrived at Stevenson.

STEVE POST: "I knew right away Ed was special. He was 6'2" or so and coordinated. When he left the gym after the first day of tryouts, I chased him down outside to make sure he was coming back the next day."

Steve attributes his prowess as coach and mentor to John Wooden, legendary UCLA coach.

STEVE POST: "I read Wooden's book, *Practical Modern Basketball*, used it as a bible. Wooden covered everything in that book, not only on-court stuff, but important off-court aspects of the game. It really guided me when I established my own program."

Summer Ball in Harlem

I didn't play much as a freshman. Our team didn't do much either. When school let out, Coach Post encouraged us to play summer basketball to refine our skills. I went to 125th Street in Harlem every day that summer. I heard about the AAU Leagues in Harlem from my buddy Anthony Lawrence. Anthony used to pick me up at the subway station every day and take me off to the courts. The guys in that league were playing at a different level. I thought the high school guys were the best players in the world. I found out that wasn't true! I was about 6'-3" at that time, and, in our age group, I was the biggest guy, so I jumped center. In our first game, I had a few inches on the guy I was jumping against. The ref tossed the ball in the air. Next thing I knew, this guy is skying over me! He kicked my ass that day! I realized I had to elevate my game just to keep up. I started working on becoming a real basketball player in that summer league.

When I went back to school that fall, Anthony Lawrence transferred to Stevenson. So did Fred Brown who played for Georgetown. All of a sudden, we had a good team.

Computer Chip Off the Old Block

What does a 14-year-old's bedroom look like when that 14-year-old is destined to star on an NCAA championship winner and play 12 years in the NBA?

I only had one poster on my wall: Walt Frazier, "Clyde." He was my hero when I was growing up. He's everything a guard should be—physical, tough, and great D. My sister Elaine gave me that poster.

Clyde was the coolest guy I could imagine—a guy who could take over a game and never panic. In that poster, he was standing by a computer. I was so taken by the fact that Clyde was on the poster, I could never remember what computer he was advertising! I'm not embarrassed about that 'cause Clyde doesn't remember either! He admitted he didn't the first time I met him. I told him I had a poster of him hanging in my room as a kid. But when I asked him what make the computer was, he couldn't remember. Great advertising, though. It got me interested in computers. I couldn't survive without a computer nowadays—and I've got Clyde and his poster to thank for getting interested.

You Scratch My Back, I'll Scratch Yours

Ed Pinckney credits coach Steve Post with giving him a good start in life, but Post puts the thanks in Ed's court.

STEVE POST: "I wouldn't have made it as a coach if I didn't start out with character kids like Ed, Anthony, and Fred. I was tentative in my early years. If I had had bad kids and troublemakers, I wouldn't have known how to stand up to them. But, those three were such good kids—respectful, obedient, and coachable.

"I have to credit Ed's family for raising him the way they did. What a difference it makes when a kid lives with a father and mother. I see it all the time. Ed's dad was a terrific guy, a hard-working man and good provider for his family. The Pinckney family was so polite. To this day, Ed's mom calls me 'Mr. Post.'

"Ed had an innocence about him. You wanted to help him. I remember a conversation I had long ago with him about playing pro basketball. He told me he wasn't interested. He thought it was phony, not real or honest like high school and college. You had to like him, for that kind of idealism and he helped me succeed as a coach."

Another Summer in Harlem

Stevenson started to jell my sophomore year. I started and we made the playoffs. That summer, I went back to Harlem and played, but I switched teams. Mr. Reese was the man who coached the team Anthony and I played for the year before—Reese's All-Stars. I thought the world of that man. I still do. But some of the other teams were doing some fabulous things—things I couldn't even imagine—like going to Greece and Europe. When Anthony and I heard about that, it was too tempting. So Anthony and I signed up for Riverside.

Giving (Back) the Shirts Off Their Backs

When Ed played for the Reese All-Stars, he couldn't afford a few changes of clothes, let alone a bag to carry his clothes in.

I just put my clothes on every day, hopped on the 35 bus, transferred to the #6 train, and headed to Harlem to play. I spent probably about two and a half hours traveling every day. I didn't bring a change of clothes. When I got to the courts, Mr. Reese—his name was Stanley Reese—handed out our uniforms. He'd haul the whole team around in his personal van to wherever we were playing. Then as soon as that last game was over, we handed everything back in to him. I never owned a basketball shirt when I was a kid.

A Star Is Born

At the start of my junior year, I wasn't a big-name player in the city. But our team was good my junior year. We played in the city semi-finals at St. John's against Benjamin Franklin High, the team that was ranked number one in the country, or at least that's what we were told at the time. These guys were awesome. I played well and we beat them. That was the big game—the semi-finals. I think we went on to win the finals by 30 points once we got past those guys.

After that game, I started to get noticed. Then when I came back senior year, I hurt my ankle in practice. It never recovered and hampered me all year. We lost to Harry S. Truman High in the first round of the playoffs. Steve Lappas was the coach. (Lappas became an assistant coach at Villanova in '84).

One on One to Up and Up

STEVE POST: "At the end of Ed's sophomore year, I made him play Fred Brown one-on-one every day after practice. What Ed needed most was to toughen up. He was too nice. I knew Ed had a competitive side. The one-on-one sessions brought it out. In the beginning, Fred cleaned him up every day. I made the loser do pushups. I think Ed got tired of doing pushups. That little competition worked. It got Ed to start fighting back, and eventually Fred and he were playing even.

"Ed came into his own in the city championships his junior year. Fred Brown was a senior and the team leader. Fred was such an intense kid, completely unlike Ed. When Fred fouled out near the end of the game, he huddled the team up, pointed to Ed and said, 'You've got to take charge now.' That's exactly what Ed did. He stepped up and played the best ball of his life. We won the city title, beating Franklin, which was, I guess you'd say, the mythical #1 team in the country. They didn't have the extensive high-school rankings they have nowadays. We won the city title that year, then lost the state title to Holy Trinity. But throughout the playoffs, Ed Pinckney stepped up and emerged as a major talent."

"In his senior year, Ed showed he had heart. He hurt his ankle early in the season, and never got back to 100 percent the rest of the year. We had to carry the poor guy off the court after the Columbus game. He wouldn't sit out though. He sat out a few practices but never missed a game. He played hurt the whole year, and still put up good numbers. His whole career, he kept moving in the right direction—up and up."

College Recruitment

Coach Post was terrific when the recruiters started contacting me. He went through the recruiting process the year before with Fred Brown and I got the benefit of his experience. The coach always had my interests at heart. He didn't feel I should go far away from my family. He gave me a process to work with. I needed that. I was getting calls and letters from exotic places everywhere, but Coach would tell me, "You're not going there." He told me in later years that he learned everything he was telling me from books. He must have read the right ones, because I wouldn't change anything about the way it all went down.

His strategy was to narrow everything down to six colleges. I picked those six with his help. I was familiar with the big basketball powers like North Carolina and Louisville. But he felt they were too far away. I did take one trip to Florida, but only because I knew two of their players from summer basketball. I had never traveled anywhere outside New York or Pennsylvania and thought it was a good chance to see someplace new. But I never seriously considered going there.

Eventually I boiled it down to Providence, Villanova, and Xavier in Cincinnati. My first choice was Providence. I liked the coach, Gary Walters. But the strangest thing happened. I had a great visit there and I was all set to accept. We were sitting in the coach's living room and he said to me, "Ed, you'll be better off going to Villanova. I think Providence is a fine school and a terrific place, but I think you'll do better at Villanova." I was floored! I never did find out why he advised me that way. But I took his advice.

Gary Walters

Gary Walters hails from Reading, Pennsylvania, where he played high school basketball under longtime Princeton coach Pete Carril. Walters attended Princeton, starting on the basketball team for three years and helping the Tigers win two Ivy League titles. Walters played on the Bill Bradley team that battled its way into the 1965 NCAA Final Four.

After college, Walters became the youngest head basketball coach in NCAA history in 1970 at Middlebury College. He followed with three years as head coach of Union College before returning to Princeton as an assistant coach in 1973.

Walters was also head coach at Dartmouth College before piloting Providence. In 1981, he left coaching entirely to join Kidder, Peabody & Co. as an investment representative. He left the firm as a senior vice president in 1990 to become senior partner of Woolf Associates Sports Management in Boston. Next he became managing director of Seaward Management, an investment advisory firm, in 1992.

Walters worked his way back to college athletics. In 1994, he was named Princeton's director of athletics and has since moved on to Kansas University. Walters serves on the NCAA Division I men's basketball committee where his duties include selection of the field for the NCAA tournament and oversight of the tournament itself.

Off to the Main Line

After my trip to Providence, I wanted to give Villanova a long hard look. I wasn't impressed my first trip. I went there thinking Villanova was a "Philadelphia school"—you know, like "a city" school. I had never been to Philly. My parents never took us outside

New York. We'd always do something in New York. They'd take us to a Broadway show or something.

Then there's the Main Line. I knew absolutely nothing about the "Main Line," the area where the Villanova campus is located. Villanova is out in the country compared to what I was used to. And the campus was a lot smaller than I expected. There wasn't a thing happening on campus when I went there the first time. All the students were gone for the holidays. I did get to meet some of the guys on the team, like Stew Granger and Alex Bradley. I liked both of them a lot. Granger was a guard—the kind of guard I respect—a very physical, tough player in and out of the lane. And Bradley was a 6'8", 245-pound muscle guy who could dominate inside. I looked at him and thought, "That'll be me when I'm a senior." I watched the team play one game, and that was about it. I went back home.

Main Line

Old Maids Never Wed And Have Babies. That little mnemonic won't get you around the Main Line, but it will help get you through it. The Main Line takes its name from the train line that runs through it. The Main Line doesn't run through Philadelphia proper, but the Main Line is packed with proper Philadelphians. It's is the high-rent district, akin to Scarsdale, Grosse Point, and other ritzy enclaves around major cities.

In 1890, the president of the Pennsylvania Railroad, George Roberts, opted to name the station stops along the Main Line railroad run after places in Wales, his country of ancestry. Trouble was, the towns along the Main Line already had names—names that Roberts chose to ignore. So he didn't call the station in Elm, Pennsylvania, "Elm," he called it "Narberth." He named the stop in Humphreysville, "Bryn Mawr," and renamed every town down the line. Eventually, the towns along the Main Line gave in, dropped their original names, and adopted the names of the train stations. It paid off, actually. Hearing Kate Hepburn brag, "I'm a Humphreysville girl you know," doesn't have the same cachet as calling herself a Bryn Mawr girl.

Anyway, take the first letter of each station stop and you wind up with that little mnemonic above: Overbrook, Merion, Narberth, Wynnewood, Ardmore, Haverford, and Bryn Mawr.

So now you're wondering, "Why isn't Villanova in that group?" Villanova is farther out (as fans from the rival St. Joe's Hawks have been saying all along), than Bryn Mawr. So, Main Liners (or whoever comes up with these silly things) invented another mnemonic for the rest of the stops.

It goes like this: Really Vicious Retrievers Snap Willingly, Snarl Dangerously. Beagles Don't, Period (Rosemont, Villanova, Radnor, St. David's Wayne, Strafford, Devon, Berwyn, Daylesford, Paoli).

Villanova has the distinction of not having had its name changed. No, Roberts was not an alumnus, but Villanova's football team knew where he lived.

Discipline

Most ballplayers avoid disciplinarians like the plague. Ed Pinckney responded more to disciplinarians than to lenient coaches. Ed recalls what drew him to Gary Walters at Providence and Rollie Massimino at Villanova.

Gary was a no-nonsense guy. He suspended three guys because their socks were longer than he allowed! That's a no-nonsense guy. Maybe it's over the top but I respect that. I think discipline builds the character of a team.

As for Rollie, I'll never forget when he came to my house recruiting. Only two coaches ever showed up at my house to recruit me: Rollie and Gary Walters. They both pulled up outside the project. The whole place knew they were coming, and everyone was peeking out the window. They both came up the stairs in three-piece suits, and both of them just looked impressive. But Rollie had a pitch that was unlike anyone else's!

Rollie walked in to my house. My mom had made some snacks. And Rollie dug in. He acted right at home. He started right off on me. "You think you're gonna walk right into my program and play? You better think again. I don't play freshman. You're not gonna start. You've got too much to learn yet, and your studies are too important. I'm gonna be on your case every day of your life about your studies. You better be at every class, and getting decent grades. Then maybe I'll play you, but you're gonna earn your way on to my team before you get out on that court."

I was thinking, "What is with this guy? I mean if I weren't gonna play, he wouldn't be coming all the way out here to see me, would he?" Rollie had a way of making people listen. You knew he was serious. And you knew he was boss.

When he left that day, my mom said, "You should go to Villanova. That little Italian coach—he'll make sure you graduate."

The Spring of '81

Ed Pinckney was no longer the star of Stevenson High. He was the guy Villanova University was pinning its future on. After high school graduation, 18-year old E-Z Ed Pinckney kissed his parents and family goodbye and settled into the Main Line campus, where that little Italian coach would make him graduate, achieve his potential, and help mold him into a champion.

Chapter Two

THE PINONE YEARS

Summer Days

Kerplunk. The Bronx inner-city kid who spent his summers on the courts in the core of the Big Apple suddenly found himself stranded on the Main Line.

I graduated, passed my college boards, and came to Villanova in the summer to take some courses. I didn't know a soul on campus or in Philly either, for that matter. All I did every day was go to class, play basketball in the Sonny Hill League, study, and work out at the Villanova gym. Mike Mulquin (Mulquin played for the Wildcats from '79–'83) was around campus that summer too. We worked out at the gym together every day and played a lot of one on one. I was so naïve. Mike was always playing hard as hell, like he was competing with me for a job. Actually he was, but I didn't know it. I didn't really know most of the guys on the team or who did what.

What I liked was that it was the first time in my life that I had a gym to hang out at. I never had a gym to go to or hang out at till Villanova. I really enjoyed that. I'd go there after classes, hang out there all the time. It gave me a chance to work on my game. I roomed at Sullivan Dorm and I'd just walk over to the gym and play when I didn't have a class.

Dwayne McClain and Gary McLain had befriended Ed at the Five Star basketball camp during their high school summers. The trio stayed in touch after the camps and wielded a lot of influence on each other's choice of college. The three had complementary styles on and off the court. Ed was the laid-back one, the easy-going big man. Dwayne was the personable guy— the graceful, athletic high flyer of the hardwoods. Gary was the energetic vocal one, the guy who dished it out good-naturedly both on and off the court. Dwayne gave Ed some other incentive for choosing Villanova.

Dwayne and his family visited Villanova one weekend when I was there. His sister was with them. She was a basketball player too. She was going to Harcum College right down the road from Villanova on the Main Line. When I saw her—well that helped my decision. She was beautiful! I figured, "This'll be great. If I go to Villanova, I'll meet lots of nice-looking girls through her."

Sonny Hill League's Biggest Guard

Ed Pinckney popped up on the Philly basketball scene as an outsider from New York.

I played in the Sonny Hill Basketball League my first summer down here, but I didn't know anyone in the League. I ran into Sonny at the Baseball Writer's Hall of Fame dinner this year, and he said the same thing he always says to me: "There's Ed Pinckney—the guard. You were a guard when you played in my league." He was right. Since I didn't know anybody, the only way I ever got the ball was to take it off the defensive glass and dribble it downcourt myself. Sonny called me the biggest guard his league ever had. I think I pulled that trick once on Rollie. He ended it right then and there: "Pinckney, I don't ever want to see you putting the ball on the floor. You get it out to Stew Granger and you get your butt upcourt quick. Running, not dribbling."

Villanova Introduction

When the students started swarming back for the fall semester, campus life heated up. Pinckney's buddies, Gary and Dwayne, joined him on campus. The trio started playing daily at the Fieldhouse. Then Villanova's basketball "preseason" started in earnest.

It was during the basketball "preseason" that I got my introduction to the guys and the coaches. We had to get up at six in the morning and report to the gym Then we'd stretch and run. I'd get up and go through the whole routine with Gary. Gary was my freshman year roomie and was always an exuberant guy. I'd be sleepy and we'd get into the gym and Gary would scream as loud as he could—and that was loud—"Let's go!" The guy could always make me laugh and forget about running. His positive attitude and clowning got me through. I hate running. I'm talking about straight running. I love to run after a basketball or a baseball. But run just to run … forget it!

Hating to run put Ed at a disadvantage in coach Rollie Massimino's program. Rollie wouldn't let anyone play until he first ran a six-minute mile. That was the ticket for admission to practice and Coach Rollie Massimino was the ticket taker.

We had to start by running a mile and then work our way up to two and a half miles. We ran those distances every day before formal practice sessions officially began. Formal practice began after the timed mile. We ran the timed mile every October 15, the day I dreaded more than all others. I'd rather go up against Ewing than face October 15. That first year, Kevin McKenna—he was a walk-on that we called Woody—kept telling everyone he was going to run his in less than five minutes. He didn't even do it in six. But neither did I. That was not a good way to start with Coach Mass. See, Coach wouldn't let a player into practice—in other words, actually play basketball—till he ran a mile in less than six minutes. When I made my time on October 16, 1981, I felt like I just won a championship ring.

Harold Jensen, one of the big heroes of the NCAA Tournament in '84-'85 arrived in Ed's junior season.

HAROLD JENSEN, Villanova player: "I had just been here about a month, and somebody got World Series tickets the night before the timed mile. I went down to the Vet with Wolfie (John Branca, a student team-manager) and we got back really late from the game. I thought, 'Great way to start, Harold.' But I did make my time.

"We did try to make the timed mile fun. We wore shirts with odds written on our backs. Pressley's jersey (Harold Pressley, who arrived Ed's sophomore year) would have 2:1 written across the back. Prez was a good runner. Eddie's odds were always high. Students would sit in the stands and watch. They'd hold signs up as you ran around. A lot of the signs listed the guy's name with his odds. They'd change the odds with each lap. In Chuck Everson's case (Chuck arrived when Ed was a junior), they held up a calendar with a different month for each lap."

Rollie admitted Ed into practice on October 16.

I went out the next day to do the timed mile again. After the first two laps, I was behind the pace I needed to break six minutes, so (coach) Paul Cormier jumped in. Paul was a dedicated runner himself. He ran the final two laps alongside me pacing me. I can still hear him encouraging me, "Keep pushing, Ed. It's all mental." I made it. I just made it, like in 5:59 or so, but it got me into practice.

All this brouhaha in the school that produced milers Eamon Coughlin and Ron Delaney.

Pumping with Mailman

Considering the extensive conditioning programs that practically every professional athletes obsesses about nowadays, it's hard to believe that, as late as the early eighties, many basketball players still shied away from weightlifting feeling it "makes you muscle-bound."

Surprisingly, I found that same belief in the NBA when I first got there. Karl Malone was the main guy who went against the tide. Karl was all about weightlifting. He practiced what he preached. He was always working out and it obviously paid off. I think Karl is 40 and he's still a star. I wish I'd have done more bodybuilding. It would have extended my career.

Life as a Freshman

Ed soon wondered why he had been so anxious to get into practice.

I walked into that first practice and saw buckets all over. Buckets ... I'm wondering, "What's all this about? Why do they have buckets on the floor?" Then I realized they were there in case anyone had to throw up. That's how hard they worked us. Nonstop. We ran weaves, suicides—run, run, run, all the time. And one of the guys did throw up that day. After practice, I think I was a little shell-shocked. I kept thinking I'd never seen anything so intense. Basketball was always just basketball to me, not conditioning. But the conditioning paid off, not only physically but mentally. Our teams always felt we had more gas left than the opponent at the end of a game. It gave us the boost we needed to come back when we were down late in a game.

In his first session, Ed found out quickly whose team Villanova's was.

Our first practice session with the varsity was something. We freshmen played the guys who had played together the year before. Everybody knows I'm sort of a quiet guy. Gary is not. Gary had this thing—he kept going on about the freshman team "setting the standard." Well, Dwayne, Gary, and I go up against the varsity in a scrimmage for the first time, and we get the ball on a fast break. I'm running upcourt on the wing. Gary spots me and gets me the ball around the circle. I figure I'm gonna make a statement. I'm competing at the next level now, beyond high school, playing on a top college team. So I go strong to the basket figuring I'm gonna dunk the ball over John Pinone. But Pinone wasn't thinking the same way. I take off in the air. Next thing I know Pinone tosses me to the ground, and I'm looking up at him, dazed. Then I hear: "You ain't dunkin' on me!"

We became good friends after that, and I gained a lot of respect for one of the hardest-nosed guys I ever saw—smart and hard-nosed. And no, I never did try to dunk over him again!

John Pinone

John Pinone was the big name in Villanova hoops when Ed Pinckney came to town in 1981. Pinone had been a star at South Catholic High in Wethersfield, Connecticut. He went on to be one of only six Wildcats to score over 2,000 points. His #45 jersey is retired. Pinone is the only Wildcat in history to lead his team in scoring average as a freshman.

His work ethic was an inspiration to his mates. His court intensity was fabled and feared. Villanova was acknowledged as "Pinone's team" for Pinone's entire career, which included Ed's freshman and sophomore years. The big New Englander was the leader and the go-to guy.

I don't know if there's another John Pinone. He was a smart player besides being so physical. Jay Wright (current coach of the

Wildcats) and I met one of his old high school coaches and we were talking about John. The guy kept emphasizing that John just naturally knew how to do things on the court—things like posting up and establishing rebounding position. What impressed me was that John knew how to do those things successfully at every level: high school, college, and pro. When I got to the NBA, I was talking to some other guys about John. They'd say, "Man, that guy was dirty." I'd say, "No, he wasn't dirty." But he was rough. All I can say is, I'm glad I didn't have to play against him. I guess that's another reason I'm happy I came to Villanova.

John Pinone set a good example for the young Pinckney about hard work, intensity, and leadership—lessons that proved valuable when Ed took over the leadership role two years later.

STEVE POST: "I traveled to as many Villanova games as I could to watch Ed. I still come down for games. Ed's right. Villanova was Pinone's team for Eddie's first two years. Pinone taught Ed a lot about toughness on the court, same as Fred Brown did in high school. And John was good for Ed in other ways. Ed was a big name for Villanova to land out of high school. Pinone was recruited heavily too, but a step below Ed. People might have expected too much too soon from Ed. Pinone helped ease that pressure. That helped Ed's development substantially."

Chuck Everson was a freshman in Pinone's senior year. Pinone left a lasting impression on Chuck too.

CHUCK EVERSON: "John Pinone gave me my greatest lesson in sport—maybe in life too. When I was a freshman, we were scrimmaging at practice. It got rough, and Pinone and I were going at it pretty good. I think I took an elbow, and started to push him. Nothing really happened because everyone stepped in and broke it up. After practice, I saw John downstairs. He said, 'You know, just forget what happened. It wasn't a big deal.' He asked if I wanted to go out for a pizza, so we did. We had a great talk, ate lots of pizza, and came back to campus. When we split up to head back to our dorms, John

John Pinone starred for the Wildcats when Ed Pinckney was a freshman and sophomore. His brother Steve later played and coached for Villanova. (Photo courtesy of the Villanova Sports Information Department)

warned me, 'Chuck, you know, tomorrow at practice, it's back on.' Once you got out on that court, that's the way it was with John. All bets were off."

Ed Pinckney Meets His Match

Ed Pinckney arrived at Villanova at a tumultuous time for the sport program. The University was dropping football that autumn, its longest-standing sport tradition. Ironically, the decision to drop the program occurred in the wake of Howie Long's graduation. Howie is Villanova's greatest football player ever. With apologies to Eagle fans, Brian Westbrook is off to a jackrabbit start, but he's got to run all the way to Canton if he wants to wrest those laurels from Howie.

I had spent the summer on campus, practically by myself. Now everybody was back. There was a big party going on because football was being dropped. I was walking up the steps on my dorm, and this girl was running out. She saw me and turned around and said there was a party over at another dorm. She told me I ought to come over. I went up to my room. I'm not really much of a beer drinker, and I'm sort of a quiet guy. But I heard all the noise from the party and I couldn't study, so I headed over. I think I only stayed about five minutes. As I was leaving the party, she stopped me and said, "Leaving already?" I didn't get the chance to talk to her too much. Then in the second semester, I had a philosophy class with her. She was an upperclassman and a cheerleader.

"She" became Rosemarie Pinkney. Rosie was a Cherry Hill, New Jersey native. She and Ed started to date that semester and ended up getting married after Ed graduated. The Pinckneys have three children: Shea, Austin, and Andrea.

Stiff Competition

The Pinone-Pinckney rivalry wasn't the only one in those intense Villanova practice sessions. Stewart Granger was a junior guard, the quarterback of the Wildcat offense. He ranks second among Villanova's all-time assist leaders, and ended up drafted in the first round by the Cleveland Cavaliers. The arrival of Gary McLain brought him face to face with a brash young challenger. The two waged a friendly but relentless competition for the next two years.

Gary and Stew competed nonstop at every level, in everything—not only in basketball, but for grades, women, video games, their looks, everything. It was a healthy competition and made each of them better. Even in the October 15 timed mile, the two of them would be at the head of the pack, running all out to win but most of all, to beat each other. I'd be dead last with a couple of the other big guys. We just trudged around the track and watched the two of them kill each other.

The Lone Granger

Stewart Granger had a great career at Villanova. He averaged 12.8 points per game as a sophomore, and 11.6 as a junior. In his junior year, he also dished out 183 assists and had 58 steals. In his senior year, the Wildcats waged a "Stew Granger for All American" campaign.

CRAIG MILLER, assistant sports information director: "We had a modest budget, but we tried to hype some of our guys for All-American. We ran a neat campaign for John Pinone. We used something like blueprint paper for a background, obviously to emphasize Pinone's workmanlike qualities. But the All-American campaign that was most fun was Stew Granger's.

We called it 'The Lone Granger.' We shot a picture of Stew on a horse on a farm outside Villanova. Stew had never been on a horse before. The horse started walking and Stew had no idea how to stop him. I don't know how many shots we had to take before finally getting one where Stew didn't look terrified!"

You Mean Everybody Does This?

Stew Granger was a big star who played with John Pinone when Ed Pinckney was a freshman and sophomore. (Photo courtesy of the Villanova Sports Information Department)

I got a big psychological edge from our conditioning program—out running every day, doing the crunches, and prepractice conditioning exercises that we did. I'd never gone through anything that rigorous before. I thought Villanova was the only team in the country doing all that—that we had a big edge on all the competition.

That notion didn't last long. My bubble burst the first Big East game we played against Boston College. Those guys were obviously doing something for conditioning! They pressed the whole game and never got winded. That gave me incentive to keep working hard all the time. Against competition at that level, you need to keep in top shape, especially when you're playing in tournaments. The best-conditioned teams have the most success in tournaments, because you have to play games on consecutive days. Rollie always made his teams tournament-tough.

Blowouts Start the '81-'82 Season

Ed's first college game was a blowout. 'Nova doubled Monmouth, 96-48.

That first game was great. I was nervous when I got in, but Stew Granger got me over it quick. I was running down the side of the court on a break and Stew just kind of glanced over. I knew instinctively what he had in mind. He lofted an alley-oop pass and I got up and jammed it. It made me feel like I belonged and could compete at this level. It also showed me again the value of a great guard who can make those plays happen.

I was nervous about that dunk. Rollie was not a guy who liked dunks. He always told us: "You dunk and miss, you're out!" I was relieved when that ball caught the nets.

The starting lineup for the opener did not include any freshmen.

Rollie told me when he was recruiting me that I wouldn't start freshman. That wasn't Rollie's system or philosophy. I didn't really expect to start. But we went back after the game and watched the films—the three of us. The films at that time were on old 8 mm reels. Dwayne kept saying, "Look, we should be starting!" We played pretty good games, and we had been gaining more and more confidence during the scrimmages, and really thought we were outplaying the starters. Dwayne said, "I'm gonna go talk to Coach Mass," So all three of us headed over to his office. Dwayne said, "Coach, I think we should be starting." Coach Mass took Dwayne into his office and shut the door. Dwayne and I did start from then on. But Coach Mass was all over us at practice. He made us earn everything from then on.

The Wildcats swept through their first six opponents: Monmouth, St. Francis, Boston College, Providence, Pennsylvania, and Towson State. They won by a combined 155 points for an average victory margin of more than 25 points. Their closest game came against Providence whom they trounced 65-54. Ed also got his first taste of Penn's legendary Palestra.

My first impression of the Palestra was that it was incredible. I remember driving up and seeing all the guys selling soft pretzels outside. I didn't know soft pretzels were such a big Philadelphia thing. I remember seeing the ticket windows for the first time, going up there on the way into the locker rooms and making sure they had tickets for my family or friends. Then I got inside and thought, "There have to be better accommodations than these!" The place was so old! There was like one shower. But as for playing on that court—what a thrill! It was just awesome with that Philly crowd. I was a NY guy. I didn't know about the Big Five and its traditions. I walk out on the floor and see all the guys on the Penn team with their heads shaved and the crowd going wild. I never played in front of such craziness. I'll never forget the first time I saw those streamers come down after the first basket. I didn't know about all those traditions. It sure made the game seem special.

Villanova was cruising through the season. Then they met a buzzsaw in Temple, who defeated the high-flying 'Cats, holding them to 48 points—their eventual season low. It was a dramatic fizzle for a Villanova five that had topped 90 in three of their first six victories. It was also Ed's first encounter with a guy who would turn out to be one of his bigger nemeses over the next four years, Temple's Granger Hall.

The 'Cats rebounded with their biggest victory margin of the season. In fact, their 121-64 pasting of Pace was the largest victory margin ever in the Pinckney era. It was the following game, however, that turned out to be one of Pinckney's most memorable.

The 'Cats Topple Bobby Knight's Indiana Team 63-58

The Indiana game was my first game at Madison Square Garden. That was a thrill in itself. I wasn't a big student of college basketball at that time, but I sure knew who Bobby Knight was. I'd glimpse over at the sidelines as the game wore on and watch him get more and more upset. We did everything right that night. It was a big confidence boost to beat a team so highly regarded nationally. I got the feeling we could compete at the highest levels that night.

In the next game, Villanova underscored the roller coaster nature of their performance—a characteristic of the entire Pinckney era.

We played St. John's next and they beat us. We just had this thing with St. John's the whole four years I was here. Maybe it was because we knew these guys all our lives, or maybe it was that Big East mystique. Anyway, when I was in high school, the guy who was the best player in our conference was on the bench. Another guy named Russell was starting ahead of him. It got me to thinking, "How good must this Russell guy be?" Anyway, we had a flat performance and they beat us.

Squeakers

Villanova's next six games, in contrast to the six at the start of the season were all squeakers against five Big East foes and Notre Dame. Three games were decided by one point, three others by a pair of points. The only loss of the six came against Connecticut.

Notre Dame was always a tough game. We hated to hear that "Notre Dame of the East" tag they tried to hang on Villanova. We believed we were just as good a school academically, and certainly as good in basketball. We went out to South Bend and beat them 48-46, but then we went up to Connecticut and lost 53-51.

The only salvation about that Connecticut loss was visiting the Pinones. Pinone's parents used to bring the whole team over to eat dinner at their house. Mrs. Pinone would prepare a huge Italian dinner in their basement. We'd eat and everybody would watch a game on TV. That happened all four years. John played my first two years, then Steve Pinone was with us the next two.

Still licking their wounds from the Connecticut loss, the Wildcats prepared to take on the feared Georgetown Hoyas for the first time.

Boola Boola, Hoya Saxa, and Blue Jays— on the Origins of the Hoya

Yale was prepping for a football game against Harvard in 1900. Alan M. Hirsh from the class of 1901 composed a nonsense ditty based on a popular song of the time, "La Hoola Boola." Basically, boola boola was gibberish, simply a euphonious phrase to sing. Hirsh posted the song on a tree near the stadium on November 24, 1900. When Yale blew Harvard out 28-0, the Eli faithful stormed the field singing "Boola Boola." So the legend is wrong. Cole Porter, a Yale class of 1913 grad, did not write "Boola Boola." Porter did write two other Yale songs, "Bull-Dog" and "Bingo, That's the Lingo," but the less acclaimed Alan Hirsh is the "Boola Boola" guy.

Meanwhile, down in D.C. ... the origin of the term Hoya is not so definitively nailed down. In some distant past when Georgetown sport teams were nicknamed "The Stonewalls" (possibly a more appropriate term for Georgetown's stoic game faces in the eighties), every Georgetown student was required to study Greek and Latin. Some as-yet-unidentified student put his Greek and Latin studies to use, and started the chant, "Hoya Saxa!" The Georgetown Athletic Department translates that as "What Rocks!" Now that cheerleaders have made the scene, that particular translation could lead to some other unintended, or intended, interpretations.

Georgetown's baseball team was nicknamed the Blue Jays in the Forties. The Philadelphia Phillies of the early Forties were perennial doormats in the National League. Years ahead of their time, they came up with what corporations do nowadays. The Phils changed their name from Phillies to Blue Jays, figuring a name change would somehow magically erase the past, wipe the slate clean, and make them suddenly competitive.

So what does Georgetown have to do with that story? Well, the Phils got a seething diatribe from Georgetown in a three-page letter of protest claiming that the Georgetown baseball team owned the name Blue Jays and the Phillies could not use it. I don't know how Johnny Cochrane or Alan Dershowitz would call that one, though it would probably depend on who was paying more. Perhaps the renown of the Georgetown Law School scared the Phils off. They never contested the point simply because the name Blue Jays never caught on in Philly. Good, bad, or indifferent, to their fans, the Phillies were and would always remain the Phillies. Ironically, Georgetown chose to forsake the name Blue Jays themselves. They eventually adopted the name Hoyas for all their teams. Besides, Hoya rhymes better with "paranoia," or "will annoy ya" as opponents see it.

The First Hoya Experience

I remember my first trip down to the Capitol Center. It's dark in there, and Georgetown wore those gray and blue sneakers. There was tension all week before that game. That's the way it always was. You worried about whether you could get the ball upcourt past their press. Georgetown wasn't just out to beat you, they were out to annihilate you. That was their style. I walked onto the court that night, and went up to Fred Brown, my good friend and high school teammate. I said hi. Fred didn't say a word, nothing—just had his game face on and stared. Even after the game, I went over to talk with him. They wouldn't let me in the Georgetown locker room. I passed John Thompson in the hall. Coach Thompson had spoken at my high school. I knew him. He didn't say hello either. I knew at that point, "This Georgetown thing is intense."

The Hoyas kicked butt, 72-56. The Wildcats revved up after the Georgetown loss with a wild 117-82 shellacking of LaSalle before returning to the Palestra for an 84-64 butt-kicking by St Joe's. Then after Georgetown again toppled them

83-72 at home, 'Nova rattled off six straight regular-season wins as Maine, Seton Hall, St. John's, Syracuse, Connecticut, and Providence all fell. The 'Cats were headed into the Big East Tournament with a full head of steam.

The Big East Tournament, '82

Tournament time as a freshman is an eye-opener. All season long, Coach Mass never really talked about tournament seedings. At the Big East Tournament, that changed. He was all about winning so we could get a good seed in the NCAA Tournament. He kept drilling into us that we had to get more focused as a team. The way we had been playing—winning six straight, I didn't know how that was possible! I found out it was.

Villanova had rolled to an 11-3 Big East record to cop the number-one seed. The '80-'81 'Cats had made a great showing the previous year. They lost an 83-80 triple-overtime heart-thumper to Syracuse. John Pinone and Alex Bradley each made the All-Tournament squad.

In the '81-'82 Big East Tournament, Villanova started positively, pounding Seton Hall, 88-73 in the first round. Then after a 74-71 squeaker over Boston College, the 'Cats met Georgetown, and for the third and final time that season, the Wildcats watched the Hoyas leave the court victorious.

That Big East Tournament my freshman year was the first time in my life I was openly criticized by the press. We were seeded number one. But then Georgetown blew us out 72-54. The media was on me. It really hit me kind of hard. I never experienced that kind of criticism or scrutiny before.

The NCAA Tournament, '82

Villanova landed a spot in the NCAA finals, and drew a first-round bye. In the second round, they won a triple-overtime thriller over Northeastern, 76-72 at the Nassau Coliseum.

I thought we were in for an easy game. Everyone was telling me you have to take your game to another level in the NCAAs. They were so right. Every shot is important. You feel it out there. We'd get back in the huddle and everyone would be screaming—the coaches and the guys too. It was so different from the regular season. My mom was at the game that night. She couldn't stay for the whole game. She was too nervous. My sister had to take her home early. Northeastern's big star was a friend of Dwayne's. What a show he put on. Watching him work taught me a lot about NCAA Tournament play. It taught me I had to bring my whole game. I kept thinking, "This guy is not going to lose this game. We've got to get the ball last and score to beat them. Or he'll beat us."

We did pull the game out. Then we played Memphis State in the Eastern regional semifinals at Raleigh, North Carolina. We needed overtime in that game, too, but ended up on top 70-66. Memphis State had Keith Lee who was more highly touted than me. I went into that game feeling I had something to prove. That's not like me normally, but I liked winning that game.

In the eastern regional finals, the Wildcats took on North Carolina with a guy named Michael Jordan on the squad.

I knew about Michael Jordan. We had played in a McDonald's game at the Cap Center and MJ scored 34 and won the MVP trophy. I saw Michael at Five Star camp in high school too, but we had never played against each other. Michael wasn't the whole show. NC had Sam Perkins and Matt Doherty who had beaten me at Stevenson High two years earlier.

We felt confident going into the game, but it seemed like, once we got out on the court, every time we missed, NC scored on a fast-break dunk. I remember one play—an alley-oop to Michael. He catches it in mid-air, Pinone grabs him, but somehow MJ spins

*around and gets a shot off. It didn't go in, but all I could think was,
'I didn't just see that move! That could not have happened!" After
that, we kind of came undone. Each guy tried to make his own
impact. On one play, I went up for a dunk. I was way over the rim,
and all of a sudden, I saw two hands—one was James Worthy's, the
other's Sam Perkins. There was a photo of the play in the Raleigh
papers next day. All you could see were arms. That's the game where
I found out that, when you lose in the NCAA Tournament, it's like
someone punched you in the stomach.*

NC downed the Wildcats 70-60 to end their season.
Personally for E-Z Ed, the Tournament was a success. His 10
Rebounds per Game average (30 boards in three games) were
the highest rebounding average in the Tournament. The team
too could take solace. The NCAA final pitted the team that
had shortstopped them in the Big East Tournament against the
team that dumped them out of the NCAA Tournament.

*Watching Georgetown and NC was an awesome feeling. I
looked back over the year after that game, and couldn't wait to start
the next year, couldn't wait to do it all over again.*

No Sophomore Jinx

Before his second year, Ed tore up his knee playing in a summer league in New York. He was hobbled when he reported to
campus that fall. He tried to play but had too much pain. He
went to an orthopedic surgeon who operated.

*I wish I had a better understanding of everything in my early
years. That team my sophomore year should have gone all the way.
I got hurt playing in a summer league, but I shouldn't have been
playing summer ball in the first place. I just didn't "get it" at that
point.*

We had such a great squad my sophomore year. If that team played our '85 championship team, the '82-'83 team would have won ten games of ten.

It was a great learning year for me. Pinone, Mulquin, and Granger were seniors. They were a tight, seasoned nucleus like Dwayne, Gary, and me would grow into. Three key guys in each class—that's a good formula for a program. I knew Pinone and the other seniors were pumped up for their final year. They were very aware that this season was their last chance.

Knit-Picking

You can't believe everything you read, at least not in the Villanova media guide. In his sophomore year, Ed Pinckney used the media guide to scam Craig Miller.

CRAIG MILLER: "I was the guy who had to gather information for the media guide. In Eddie's sophomore year, he told me his hobbies were 'woodcrafting and knitting.' It kind of surprised me, but then I thought, 'Hey, Ed has so many sisters. Who knows? And if a big guy like Rosey Grier was into knitting, maybe Ed picked it up somewhere along the way too.' But Ed was playing a joke on me and I didn't catch it. E-Z Ed got me."

Starting the '82-'83 Season

Villanova was impressive on paper. They hoped to better their 24-8 mark from the previous season. Pinckney and Dwayne McClain tucked a year of experience under their belts. The squad had been bolstered by the addition of highly touted, heavily recruited Harold Pressley. Pressley was a consensus high school All-American and a three-time All Stater from Connecticut. Dwight Wilbur, a slashing, penetrating guard, was another quality addition. Pressley was immediately pressed into the starting lineup.

Dwayne and I always joked about that. Prez came in as a freshman and was penciled right into the starting lineup from pre-season on. We thought Rollie didn't start freshmen! At least, that's what he told us when we first got there.

Full of optimism for a banner season, the Wildcats limped out to a tepid 2-2 start. One of those losses came at the hands of national-power Kentucky, who proved the real Wildcat that night.

We were full of ourselves. We lost bad to Kentucky, 93-79, on national TV. At the time, I didn't know much about the Kentucky legacy or mystique. But they were focused that night. They were all business. So was Penn when they upset us in the next game. We're expecting great things and we start out 2-2. I believe we were all thinking, "This is going to be easy this year!" because of all the success we had the year before.

ROB WILSON ("STATS"), team manager: "We were flat that game. I felt bad for Harold Pressley. He had just come to Villanova with a big high school reputation and I know he was a bit nervous. He threw up a few airballs that game on national TV, and it took a while for him to recover his confidence."

Ten Straight

Villanova worked out of its tailspin by reeling off ten straight victories, the longest victory skein in the Pinckney years. In the midst of the streak, they won the Cabrillo Classic in San Diego, topping both Tulsa and San Diego State.

That was our first real trip, except for Raleigh in the NCAAs and Hartford at the Big East Tournament. The trip was lots of fun, but the best thing was that we stayed focused and played well. That's when Rollie really started his talk about going to the NCAA finals in New Orleans that year. He kept yelling, "There's gonna be 60,000 screaming people out there. Do you know what it's like to play in front of all those people? Are you gonna be ready, Pinckney?"

The Prez

When Prez (Harold Pressley was known as Prez or Coz because he resembled Bill Cosby—facially, not comedically) came as a freshman, we went up against Boston College at the Meadowlands. Prez had turned down BC to come to Villanova. The stands were full, and every time Prez touched the ball, the whole crowd would do that mocking chant, "Har-rold, Har-rold." Prez was a big high school star up in New England, and the BC fans were really angry that he didn't choose BC. They really resented when he came to Villanova. He had a terrible game and it really hurt his mental game for a while.

Defeating Georgetown

The Wildcats' ten-game romp was broken by arch-nemesis St. John's who outscored the 'Cats 80-71. Another setback followed when Syracuse outpointed the 'Cats 83-75 at the Palestra. The two defeats set the stage for one of Ed Pinckney's finest hours. The Hoyas had rocked the Wildcats three times the previous year. But on January 31, 1983, the Wildcats registered their first ever Big East Conference win over Georgetown, 68-67. Pinckney netted 27 and grabbed 22 rebounds, while Ewing managed only eight points. David Wingate topped the

Hoyas' scorers with 16 as Georgetown led most of the night. Villanova hung in, however, and surged ahead with eight seconds remaining to pull off a thrilling upset.

We had a pep rally on campus before the Georgetown game. I was at the microphone and said something like, "Don't worry about Ewing. I'll take care of him." I walked away thinking, "What did I just say?" We played them and the pace was really fast, almost playground style. We all played well. Pinone had a great game. I was sick that game, but my knee was feeling good for the first time all season. It was a real confidence booster to beat them. These were the guys we watched on TV playing for the national championship the year before. Our team was so inconsistent, though. After that Georgetown high, the very next game BC wound up beating us. I played horribly. They had a freshman, Roger McCready, a 6'5", undersized guy, a pit bull, and I couldn't get started. That inconsistency would drive Coach Mass nuts. I'd tell him, "I can't explain it, Coach. The shots just didn't go in tonight." That wasn't good enough for him.

After shaking off the BC loss at the Meadowlands, the streaky Wildcat five strung together seven straight wins. Their 56-53 win against national champ North Carolina in the middle of that streak remains one of the school's most glorious.

ROB WILSON ("STATS"): "Pittsburgh was in town early for the game. They were staying nearby in Radnor. It started to snow heavily the day of the game but Pittsburgh got here with no problem because Radnor's right down the road from Villanova. The students were supposed to start finals that day, but with the snow, classes were canceled. Students everywhere recognize that as a signal to start partying, which they did, beginning early in the day. By game time, that gym was wilder than I've ever seen.

Of Saints and Suds

Villanova's patron saint, St. Augustine, must have been watching over the fans at that Pitt game. Since the weather outside was frightful and college students by definition need little excuse to tap a keg, it was a banner day for Villanova purveyors of suds. No matter. St. Augustine Villanova University's patron saint also happens to be the patron saint of brewers. Why? Because he himself left behind a life of debauchery before dedicating himself to a life of service to God. No one knows if anyone in the stands had a life-changing experience that day—other than giving them more time to study for finals that were postponed.

A Big Win in Chapel Hill

We beat Pitt pretty easily, 78-65. And it kept on snowing. Next day, we were all in Rollie's office watching the Notre Dame game on TV. The announcers were rambling on that there was bad weather back east, and Villanova might not be able to make it down to play North Carolina for the nationally televised Sunday game. They added, "But Digger Phelps has agreed to extend Notre Dame's stay in Carolina and play NC if Villanova gets snowed in." Rollie hit the roof! He was determined not to let that happen. We found a bus company that could get us there in time—after a 12-hour ride. Rollie's staff kept working to find a better alternative. Philly airport was closed, but Dave Coskey found that the airport in Atlantic City New Jersey was open. He located a prop plane that could get us down there in five hours or so. Actually, that was the first time I ever flew. We took a bus down to Atlantic City, boarded the plane, and checked into the hotel late, at about 1 a.m. Next day, we had a walk-through practice in the parking lot.

I think NC had a ten-year winning streak against nonconference rivals at home at the time, but we avenged the loss in the NCAA Tournament the previous year.

I started off great in the North Carolina game. Worthy graduated the year before. He had gotten hurt and was sitting on the sideline. I was looking over at him during the timeouts. But I hurt my ankle that game, and Mulquin came in. He played great. Everyone was happy for Mike. I learned from his performance that you always have to be ready. Well, Mike was ready and he helped us win that game.

So on February 13, 1983, two weeks after the euphoria of the Georgetown upset, the 'Cats upended Michael Jordan and his number-one ranked, defending national champion Tar Heels, 56-53, in Chapel Hill on national TV. It was the first time in history Villanova ever beat North Carolina. Though Pinckney was hurt, he managed 11 points and 11 boards to complement Pinone's 14-point, seven-rebound performance. Jordan answered with 20, while teammate Sam Perkins pitched in 15 in a losing effort.

E-Z Bear

The Pinone-Pinckney tandem was getting a bit of media attention because of their big wins. Apparently, it wasn't quite enough.

CRAIG MILLER: "I had to pick up Al McGuire (McGuire had coached Marquette from 1968-1977) at the airport in Philly. He was broadcasting one of our games here. Al gets in the car, his hair all disheveled from the flight and rushing through the airport. He gets in and says, 'So, Craig, tell me about Ed Pinckney the Bear, and E-Z John Pinone.' I said, 'Do you ever have that backwards! No one would ever accuse

Pinone of being E-Z.' And Eddie was so skinny back then, no one would ever call him 'The Bear.' Once McGuire saw them play, he got it straight."

History Repeats and
Phi Slamma Jamma Jams

The 'Cats rolled over Providence, Connecticut, and St. Joe's before history—all too recent history—repeated itself. Just as consecutive losses to St. John's and Syracuse halted their earlier 10-game streak, the Wildcats' seven-game streak jolted to a halt compliments of the same two culprits. Georgetown added a third straight loss to the tailspin as the 'Cats prepared for the Big East Tournament.

The number-two seeded 'Cats eked out a one-point win over Connecticut, 69-68, before getting ousted, 91-80, by St. John's in the second round. Despite the Big East Tournament loss, Villanova was invited to the NCAA Tournament for the fourth consecutive year. They followed a first-round bye with a 60-58 heart-thumper over Lamar in Houston, Texas. They headed next to Kansas City where they squeaked by Iowa 55-54 in the Midwest Regional Semifinals. Iowa's coach was George Raveling, who starred for 'Nova from '57-'60, and retains the tenth slot, all time, among Wildcat rebounders. That was the extent of the Wildcat march. They were eliminated emphatically 89-71 by Houston's Clyde Drexler-led Phi Slamma Jamma. Just as Villanova had done the previous year, they watched the team that ended their March Madness battle for the national title. Houston ended up losing to NC State in one of the NCAA's greatest upsets.

ROB WILSON ("STATS"): "Rollie was going nuts at the officials in that Houston game. He was waving his arms so much on this one call that his glasses fell to the floor and he stomped on them. Rollie never saw them and never knew what happened to them."

Iowa had two good players, Greg Stokes and Michael Payne. I knew I needed a good game against these guys. I had a good game, and we still just squeaked by. We were rolling right along, feeling too confident against Houston. Even Pinone was. Villanova had blown Houston out 90-72 in the 1981 NCAA Tournament. But this Houston team was not the same team as that one. I knew we were in trouble when I watched Houston beat Memphis State. I saw Clyde Drexler sky over two guys and jam the ball, and I thought, "Ooh, these guys are trouble." They were! We had some great athletes on our team like Dwayne, but no one who could match what I saw Drexler do. Anyway, I don't think we could have beaten Houston with the mindset we had that year. Gary, Dwayne, and I were too cavalier and too inconsistent. We were the main culprits.

Phi Slamma Jamma sounded the death knell to the Pinone years. Pinone left with some personal satisfaction. He had the highest free-throw percentage in the NCAA Tournament, hitting 15 of 15 tries in the competition. However, it was no longer Pinone's team. It was E-Z Ed's. The baton was passed.

Chapter Three

THE BATON IS
PASSED

Pinckney's Junior Year

The baton was now officially passed from the Pinone-Granger contingent to the Pinckney-McLain-McClain trio.

We had high expectations. We were coming off two consecutive 24-8 seasons, and two consecutive Final Eights in the NCAAs. Prez with a year under his belt, and Harold Jenson was coming in with a big reputation from high school. But I tell you, I'll bet I was the worst prepared leader in the country. After everyone was used to Pinone and Granger as leaders, I come along as a leader who says nothing. Those guys were vocal leaders, aggressive. Gary, on the other hand, was up to the challenge of leadership. With Stew gone, Gary's feeling like, "I finally got control." And he did just that. Gary took control. Rollie worked with the three of us daily on leadership and what our roles had to be.

The Wildcat season opened with a 57-50 overtime win over Big Five archrival, St. Joe's at the Palestra. After a 78-50 laugher

Ed Pinckney and Dwayne McClain (above) were friends from high school basketball camp who partnered for four years at Villanova. (Photo courtesy of the Villanova Sports Information Department)

over Loyola of Maryland, the 'Cats were upended by Temple and LaSalle in two Palestra tilts. The 2-2 start matched the weak start of the previous season. But things were about to get worse. When the team headed south, so did the season.

The Wildcats played in the UAB Classic in Birmingham where Alabama (UAB) prevailed 78-76 in a triple OT final. The 'Cats packed their bags and zipped down to Jacksonville, Florida, for the Gator Bowl Tournament. They suffered two straight losses at the hands of Jacksonville and Auburn, with its "Round Mound of Rebound," Charles Barkley.

'Nova dragged its three-game losing skid home only to see it stretch to five as Syracuse and Boston College downed the Wildcats. Villanova found itself languishing at 3-7, the first and only losing record during the Pinckney era.

We couldn't get started. We played a really tough Temple team with Granger Hall. I always had trouble with him. I figured I needed a good game. That would appease Rollie. Well, I did. Trouble was, so did Granger and we lost. Then we got to Florida and weren't focused. We were more focused on what we were going to do at Disneyworld and that's the way we played—distracted. When we got back, our heads were spinning. Rollie tried to get Frank Dobbs to step up as the team leader and get Gary, Dwayne and me on track. That was tough though. Frank was just a student like us, so it was a tough role for him to take on.

Frank was actually the best choice to fill that role. He was one of the few guys that had a car on campus. Frank was mature. I guess that's how I'd describe him—a great influence on me and the younger guys. When I first got to Villanova, Stew, Aaron Howard, Gary, and I used to pile into Frank's car to drive down to the Palestra.

I grew a lot because of those guys. They all seemed to be in control of everything in their lives: academics, social life, and sports. Especially Frank. They all commanded respect, but not only as athletes. They had respect around campus. They had relationships with people outside of sports. They were way ahead of me that way, and I learned a lot just watching them operate.

Even with all that, it was still tough for Frank to try to make Gary, Dwayne, and me better leaders.

Downing the Hoyas Again and More Inconsistency

The Wildcats continued their inconsistent, streaky ways by rolling to three consecutive victories. The biggest was a double-overtime toppling of the Hoyas in their own Capital Center lair. It was the first time Villanova ever bested Georgetown on the road in Big East play. Countering Patrick Ewing's 14 point, 15-rebound effort, Harold Pressley came up big, tallying 17. Pinckney wasn't far behind with 16. Just as the 'Cats had done the previous season, they fell flat after beating Georgetown. For the first time in three seasons, Notre Dame beat the 'Cats, who failed to climb back up to .500 with the loss.

CHUCK EVERSON: "I had my best college game against Georgetown when I was a sophomore. I knew I had to go up against Ewing. Patrick was great, but my dad encouraged me, 'Just keep going at him.' So I did, and Patrick got three fouls and had to back off. I ended up with 13 points and six rebounds in 19 minutes. Dwayne had played against Patrick several times, and so did Eddie. Eddie had that awesome game as a sophomore with 27 points against Georgetown when he was sick.

"Generally, our whole team had more confidence against Georgetown than their other opponents had. We were proud that we played in the Big East. We were convinced it was the toughest conference in the country. It was a hard-nosed brand of ball—lots of confrontation, and when you got fouled, you got fouled hard."

We lost to a Notre Dame team that was not that good. I really started to have doubts at that point, kind of thinking: "Everybody says Pinckney is good. Maybe he's not that good." After the loss, I got more serious. We weren't even a .500 team. I practiced harder, got more vocal on the court, and I worked at elevating my game. The leaders started to get it at that point. We started to reach out to the other guys on the team, trying to help them improve. Basically, we started acting more like leaders. Like Chuck Everson and Wyatt Maker—we always joked around with those guys. We'd give it to them good, but as a leader, I figured shouldn't just joke with them. I can still have fun, but I should start trying to build up their self-confidence, help bring them along. I don't think Dwayne, Gary, and I really embraced our roles as leaders till we lost at Notre Dame.

In the wake of the Notre Dame debacle, the team woke up and zipped off six straight Ws. That six-pack included three straight Big East wins. Pitt and Georgetown hung back-to-back losses on the 'Cats before Villanova rebounded with four straight victories. They closed the regular season with their second straight one-point win over St. John's—a nifty 73-72 overtime win at the Palestra.

Villanova slipped down another slot to third in the Big East seeding. In the first round, they drubbed Pittsburgh 75-65, but Syracuse outlasted them 66-65 in the semis.

For the first time in three seasons, the 'Cats did not draw a first-round bye in the NCAA Tournament, Still they beat Marshall handily, 84-72 before falling flat in the next game when Illinois dumped them 64-56.

After we lost to Illinois 64-56 in the NCAAs, I felt bad for Frank Dobbs. He was the only senior, and I felt like we left him down.

DWAYNE McCLAIN: "You know, Rollie was so upset about that loss. We got back to campus and he made us practice. The season was over, but he had us practicing! I think I felt the same way. I thought something special was in store for us next year."

Was it ever.

Rollie Massimino presents Ed Pinckney with the game ball for his 1,000th point on January 3, 1984. (Photo courtesy of the Villanova Sports Information Department)

Chapter Four

THE CHAMPIONSHIP
SEASON GETS
ROLLING

E d Pinckney's final season got a jump start on November 28. That night Villanova ascended into the then and still exclusive club of 1,000-game winners in NCAA basketball.

Getting the school's one thousandth win was special for all of us. It was extra special for Coach Mass cause we got it agianst Vermont, which was Coach Mass's alma mater. He was a basketball player there, and at halftime, he was inducted into the University's Hall of Fame. We all ate one of Coach Mass's big Italian dinners before the game—of course that goes without saying. Coach Mass knew where all the great Italian restaurants were everywhere we went. And everywhere he took us, they'd give us the red-carpet treatment as soon as we showed up.

In front of a sellout crowd in Burlington Vermont, Pinckney topped all scorers with 15 while Pressley topped all rebounders with eight. The Villanova five moved on to Poughkeepsie to square off against Marist. The favored Wildcats suffered a scare when the home team carried a 30-27 halftime edge into the locker room, but Villanova went on to win.

The 1,000 Win Club in 1984

Villanova joined the elite list of 1,000 game winners in 1984. The list underscores the strength of Philadelphia's Big Five. In 1984, only 32 teams nationwide had reached the milestone, and four of them were Philadelphia teams. No other city could come close to that claim. Villanova was the fourth member of the Big Five to win 1,000. Only La Salle had won less than 1,000 by 1984.

Before you diss the Explorers, remember that La Salle was also the only Big Five team up to that point that ever won an NCAA championship (in 1954).

Among the 1,000-win club members, Villanova was tied for ninth in winning percentage.

TEAM	FIRST YEAR	WON	LOST	PCT.
1. Kentucky	1903	1358	423	.762
2. North Carolina	1911	1317	492	.728
3. St. John's	1908	1277	551	.699
4. Kansas	1899	1270	618	.673
5. Oregon State	1902	1258	786	.615
6. **Pennsylvania**	1902	1239	672	.648
7. Notre Dame	1898	1199	590	.670
8. Washington	1896	1185	687	.633
9. **Temple**	1895	1180	684	.633
10. Duke	1906	1176	642	.646
11. Syracuse	1901	1131	573	.664
12. Princeton	1901	1122	729	.606
13. Western Kentucky	1915	1115	498	.691
14. Indiana	1901	1108	640	.634
15. UCLA	1920	1106	485	.695
16. Washington State	1902	1101	950	.537
17. Bradley	1903	1094	652	.627
18. N. Carolina State	1913	1086	585	.650

19. West Virginia	1904	1083	665	.621
20. Purdue	1897	1072	630	.630
21. Utah	1909	1067	594	.642
22. USC	1907	1062	679	.610
23. Texas	1906	1049	679	.607
24. Illinois	1906	1046	602	.635
25. **St. Joseph's (Philadelphia)**	1912	1037	633	.641
26. Ohio State	1899	1032	707	.593
27. Louisville	1912	1030	551	.651
28. Cincinnati	1901	1024	647	.633
29. Kansas State	1905	1016	694	.594
30. Tennessee	1909	1011	582	.635
31. Dayton	1904	1010	655	.607
32. **Villanova**	1921	1000	535	.651

Potential

Potential. Ed Pinckney heard that word from Rollie Massimino endlessly. By the time he was a senior, Pinckney had hung a banner, "Fulfill your potential," in his locker.

I didn't hear "potential" from Rollie too much as a freshman and sophomore. But I started hearing it more and more in my junior year. In my senior year, I heard it non-stop, "Pinckney, you have the potential to do great things. You gotta reach for everything inside of you, and you've got to do it now."

Early Season Ups and Downs

Temple was next. The Owls posed the 2-0 'Cats with their first test of the young season.

Against Temple, I was out to redeem myself. Our guys were really working me over. I always had trouble with Granger Hall my entire career at 'Nova. The guys started riding me, "You're scared of him—and not only are you scared of him, he's better than you." They pumped me up. I played a good game, though it didn't show in the numbers, and we won. Of course, Granger played a great game too and put up even better numbers. Funny, Granger and I competed all those years in the Big Five and then I wound up drafted in the first round by the Suns, and they grabbed Granger in the second.

Dwayne McClain turned in a sterling performance with 22 points and eight rebounds. Wyatt Maker was superb in a relief role. In 17 minutes of subbing, Maker tallied 11 on four for five shooting.

The 'Cats were sailing along smoothly, winning their first seven contests. Their first loss came in the Cotton States Kiwanis Classic at the Omni in Atlanta. After they downed Brigham Young in the first game of the Classic, they blew a 29-25 half-time edge over Georgia and lost 75-68 in overtime. The game was tight till the overtime period, when four Villanova starters: Pressley, McLain, Wilbur, and Pinckney, fouled out.

I had four charges called on me. It's simple. I didn't play smart basketball. I kind of resolved from that point on that I couldn't foul out. I was supposed to be the leader of the team and I had to be the one to set the example. I think that loss helped me get a better understanding of leadership.

The 'Cats rebounded with two Big East wins, outscoring Syracuse by 12 at the Palestra and Connecticut by 11 at the Field House. The 'Cats brought their glittery 9-1 record to

Jamaica, New York where a potent second-half Red Force assault overcame a six-point Villanova halftime advantage.

The first St. John's game, Mullin hit three straight against us at one point. It was a defining moment for the year. It was like we could never catch up to those guys that year. They were always tough every year. But in my senior year, they added Walter Berry, and they were comparing him to Prez and me early in the season.

The St. John's triumvirate of Mullin, Berry, and Wennington tallied 20, 15, and 17 respectively and proved too much that night ... and that season.

Welcome to the Big East

Mark Plansky was a huge high school star in New England. He watched Big East basketball as a kid, so he was excited and nervous when he went in the St. John's game. Mark would be going up against one of the heroes he followed in high school.

MARK PLANSKY: "My debut in the Big East didn't go quite the way I imagined. I had to guard Chris Mullin. I emulated Chris in my own game. Chris was a white kid, not too fast—kind of like me, or so I thought.

"Waiting to go in, I've got cottonmouth, I'm nervous. I'm determined to play him tight and tough. Then Chris got the ball and I moved in on him. He gave a whole series of head and body fakes before going up for the shot. When he does, his elbow hits my nose. Of course the ball swishes through. I'm running down the court with a bloody nose after giving up the basket. That wasn't my dream debut!"

Mid-Season Stretch

The next game was a low-scoring, in-your-face rumble with Georgetown at the Spectrum. It took an overtime period for the Hoyas to notch a slim 52-50 victory. Georgetown turned the ball over 23 times versus only 18 for the 'Cats. D-Train McClain topped all scorers with 18. Heavy hitters Pinckney and Ewing were limited to eight and 10 respectively.

I figured I'd take a page from Mullin's book that game. I was determined to do everything myself. You can't do that against a team as disciplined and well coached as Georgetown. Their front line killed me.

In the wake of the heartbreaker against Georgetown, Villanova ran off a modest four-game winning streak. It was destined to be the longest winning streak the 'Cats could muster in the regular season. Boston College, Seton Hall, Drexel, and Providence fell in succession before 'Nova trekked south to College Park Maryland for a fray with Maryland.

In the Maryland game, Rollie had started to give Plansky and Jensen more playing time. Lenny Bias for Maryland was playing a great game, but Plansky played quite a bit. I was impressed with the way he played. He was tough, confident, and unafraid for a guy with no experience. I gained a lot of respect for Mark that game. He fouled out, but so did Lenny Bias, so Mark did his job. We lost the game, but we salvaged a minor victory. Our guys were starting to act like they believed in themselves. And at this point, not only were all the starters on the same page. So were the subs.

The 'Cats sandwiched a loss to Syracuse in between wins over Pitt and Connecticut. Then came the fall.

Rollie Aids

HAROLD JENSEN: "When we played Syracuse, the game ended late, like about 11 p.m. We had reservations for an early flight next morning at six a.m. Rollie had eaten a late-night dinner after the game. It was freezing cold up there in upstate New York. Rollie didn't show up on time. You have no idea how unusual that was for him! 'On time' to Coach Mass meant a half-hour early. We kept calling his room and finally got him. He rushed down. His hair was all disheveled and looked kind of comical. He had Italian bread under his left arm and a bag of pepperoni or something under his other arm. But believe me, no one said a word. We had lost the night before, and Coach Mass was in no mood. And he didn't feel too good, either, so we all kept our mouths shut."

Dropping Three

The low point of the campaign came with the three straight losses to St. John's, Georgetown, and Boston College.

In the 'Cats' second '84-'85 loss to St. John's, the Mullin-Wennington-Berry trio tallied 21-14-18 respectively for 53 points versus the 52 they put up in the first game. Mullin again proved the biggest 'Cat Killer. After being throttled back to four first-half points, the 6'6" senior revved up at the end, bucketing 12 of the Red Force's final 18 points. The victory, which was broadcast on the PRISM cable channel, was the 15th win in a row for St. John's. The sold-out Spectrum rocked at halftime, as the partisan Philly crowd sang "Happy Birthday" to Jake Nevin.

A St. John's Revelation for Chris Mullin

Ed Pinckney and Chris Mullin were big New York high school stars in 1981. Mullin chose St. John's, Pinckney Villanova.

Chris and I knew each other in high school. We were friends. He used to come over to my neighborhood sometimes and we'd play ball. My friends would say, "Who's that white guy? He's good!" So Chris and I go way back.

He asked me once why I went to Villanova and not St. John's. I told him it was simple. St. John's didn't recruit me. Chris couldn't believe I had played in New York and St. John's let me slip away. But they did. Chris thought St. John's would have won everything if I had been on the squad with him and Walter (Berry). Who knows? But I couldn't be happier with my choice to go to Villanova. And one thing's sure. We did win it all.

Tough Schedule

History repeats. After St. John's triumphed, Georgetown did the same. In the unfriendly confines of the Capital Centre, Villanova streaked out to a 9-0 advantage Georgetown didn't reach double figures till 12:36 into the contest. The 'Cats shot with 49-percent accuracy from the field while pressuring Georgetown into uncharacteristic 39-percent shooting accuracy. But Georgetown's four-turnover, nine-rebound advantage proved too much to overcome. After the game, Georgetown coach John Thompson pronounced prophetically, "All everybody talks about is St. John's and Georgetown, but whoever draws Villanova in the tournament is in for a rude awakening if they think they're getting a patsy."

Villanova's next loss was perhaps harder to take. They had just lost tight games to the number-one and number-two teams in the nation. Boston College on the other hand was a team the Wildcats had steamrolled earlier, 85-66. 'Nova appeared to have the game in hand with a nine-point lead and nine minutes remaining. BC, however, revived and rattled off nine unanswered points, narrowing the gap to one. The game came down to one last-second shot by D-Train that rimmed the basket and slithered out as the 'Cats' rally fell short.

'Nova's unrelenting schedule provided no relief. The Main Line hoopsters had to take on city rival St. Joe's at the Spectrum. In a game telecast by PRISM, Gary McLain provided the heroics. With four seconds showing on the clock, he swished an 18-footer from the corner and followed with a foul shot to ice a 47-44 triumph.

STEVE PINONE: "We had such a tough schedule! We played all those tough Big East games, then we come back and got St. Joe's in the Spectrum. That game was mentally draining because they could hold the ball on you, and anything could happen."

Then the 'Nova five trekked north to the Providence Civic Center to take on an emotionally charged Providence Friar squad. The Friars' coach, Joe Mullaney, had announced his resignation, and the school was honoring him in pregame ceremonies (Rick Pitino was later named as Mullaney's replacement). The two standing ovations that the vocal partisan throng of 8,707 gave their legendary coach didn't faze the 'Cats, who led from the center tip. Villanova rolled its lead up as high as 16 only to see it whittled down to one. Ultimately, Harold Pressley, who turned in a monster game, regulated. He netted six of his 25 points in the next two minutes. His effort lengthened the Villanova lead back to four and provided enough oomph to ride out the victory.

The senior trio of Ed-Gary-Dwayne came within of whisker of blemishing its perfect record at the Field House. The three seniors had never lost a game there. The seniors were cruising along on a perfect 16-0 record over their four years of play (the

Villanova streak stood at 18 wins). The final opponent at the Field House was Seton Hall, who was 0-14 in Big East play up to that point. However, the Wildcats watched their modest six-point halftime lead evaporate as the contest deadlocked at 74. Only 2:20 remained. To make matters worse, Pinckney, who had tossed in 24 points and nabbed seven rebounds, fouled out in the final two minutes. It was Prez once again who stepped up. Harold made a key block of Andre McCloud's jump shot to preserve a Villanova victory.

The Collapse

The 'Novans traveled out to Pittsburgh to conclude the regular season.

ROB WILSON ("STATS"): "We had a great meal out there. We always ate particularly well in Pittsburgh. Rollie used to take the whole team to the Italian-American Club. They'd put every Italian dish you could ever imagine out on big, long tables and we'd gorge ourselves for about three hours."

VIC D'ASCENZO, team manager: "You've got to understand—eating was a big thing to these guys! They normally ate university food from the cafeteria like every other Villanova student. When they got a chance to eat a home-cooked meal, they did a number on it, especially during school breaks when they were stuck on campus alone. Most of the guys on the team didn't have a car. I think Harold Jensen had one in his junior year or so, but practically no one else did, so transportation was difficult. Sometimes we'd all run down to South Philly for a Pat's Steak. A lot of times everybody would come to my parents' house for a good cooked meal. I didn't live too far from campus. My mom made a huge dessert once, a pudding, and Dwayne was so hungry, he ate the whole thing."

Coach Rollie Massimino talks to the second stringers at the disastrous Pittsburgh game. (Photo courtesy of the Villanova Sports Information Department)

Despite the good eatin', the trip to Pittsburgh left a bad taste. In his final regular-season game as a senior—a game that was telecast nationally by *CBS Sports*—Ed Pinckney, along with Dwayne, Gary, and the rest of the starters, found themselves in an unusual position. The starting team was on the bench for virtually the entire second half.

Villanova played the first half flatter than a wrestling mat after a week of Sumo Wrestlemania. The flatter his starters played, the more animated—no, make that agitated—Rollie got. 'Nova started off in the hole, 0-6. After they managed to narrow the gap to 14-10, things deteriorated. On national TV, the Wildcats bumbled into the locker room at halftime saddled with a 40-23 deficit. Pinckney managed only two points on 0-2 shooting, to go along with three rebounds and three fouls. Pressley shot one of seven for five points while committing two personal fouls. Dwight Wilbur shot 2-5, while Gary McLain complemented his two points with a lone assist.

ROB WILSON ("STATS"): "Rollie felt the guys were embarrassing themselves on national TV. He told the starters in the locker room—in no uncertain terms—that he was giving them three minutes to show him desire and commitment. If they didn't, he was yanking them all. He was a man of his word. Rollie could put up with anything except lack of effort and commitment, and he wasn't seeing that on the court that day. He threatened them with three minutes. I don't think he gave them two. He wasn't pleased with what he saw, so he pulled them all. I don't think he had any intention of ever putting them back in that day."

DWAYNE McCLAIN: "I was actually having a decent game! I scored 13 points in a half. But Coach Mass had taken all he could. He pulled the whole starting unit off the floor. We learned a lesson from that game."

It was embarrassing, but Coach made his point. It made us all reflect. It was a real wakeup call. I remember sitting on that bench thinking, "Here it is, Ed Pinckney's last game in his senior year, and he's sitting on the bench. What is going on?" Maybe I needed that shock going into the tournaments. But something else good came out of that incident. The subs Coach Mass put out on the court: Chuck, Harold Jensen, Connally Brown, and others all played hard. They played with confidence. All of a sudden, those guys became a big part of the team. That feeling of togetherness helped us all going into the tournament.

STEVE PINONE (sophomore on the championship team): "What a helluva time for me to go in! I hardly played all year long. Next thing I know, I'm guarding Andre Williams—a guy who's very athletic, and I'm very unathletic. The other problem was that I was in the worst shape of the year. It was late in the season, and practices had gotten less and less intense, to keep the starters fresh for the actual games. So I was really sucking air!

"You know, I'm glad I'm talking about this! I forgot. CBS owes me a trophy! You know they used to pick an MVP from each team on those broadcasts. In that game they gave the MVP award to the 'Villanova second team!' I saw one trophy around here for a while after that game, but I was told we were all supposed to get one. If that's the case, they still owe me my trophy."

MARK PLANSKY: "I really felt sorry for Steve. I just had surgery after an injury in the Boston College game, so I was the only bench player who didn't see action. When Steve went in, I could see he was struggling against a really tough guy to keep up with. But Steve ran his butt off trying!"

ROB WILSON ("STATS"): "That whole benching incident was a family matter to Rollie. He wanted to teach the kids a lesson about giving their all. He refrained from making any harsh criticism to the press—just like he would do if the players were his kids. Actually one of them was his kid (R.C. Massimino, the coach's son, was on the team). But that father-son relationship was what he tried to nurture with all of them. He saw his role as that of a strict, loving father. Rollie didn't want to embarrass anyone in the family. He told the press he pulled the starters because of match-up issues. He kept dirty laundry from the press—just like a good father would do."

Off the Chart

One day early in the season Dwayne came up to me and showed me a chart he made up—an elaborate thing, too. He had tomahawk dunks, Statue of Liberty dunks, hook dunks. You name a dunk, it was on the chart. We hung it up in the locker room. Well, we kind of put it sort of just where Dwayne and I could see it. We didn't want Rollie to spot it. Rollie was not a big fan of the dunk. Anyway, we checked off every dunk we did in a game. The goal was to check off the whole chart before we left Villanova.

Actually, Rollie should have encouraged us to chart the dunks. It was a worthwhile exercise for us. Know why? We learned a lot of basketball in the process. We used to ask the coaches for the tapes so we could watch what dunks we had done. Then we could check them off on the chart. The games were on reel-to-reel tapes at that time. While we were watching the tapes, we'd be taking everything else in too. We became a lot more analytical and we kind of understood each other's court mentality better as a result. I think that dunk chart really lifted our performance that year.

Lessons

The Pittsburgh benching underscores how Rollie Massimino practiced what he preached to his kids. Massimino's move turned out to be a much needed character builder. It was also a gutsy move. With an 18-9 record, Villanova was on the cusp—far from a cinch to receive a bid to the NCAA Tournament. Massimino was willing to jeopardize getting that bid for something he considered more valuable—teaching a lesson about life to his young charges.

The Big East Tournament

We were confident entering the tournaments. As I said, the team my sophomore year was the best I ever played on. I think that squad would have beaten the '85 championship team every time. That '83 team had John Pinone at center, Stewart Granger and Dwight Wilbur at guards, and me, Harold Presley, and Mike Mulquin at forward. Gary was a point guard, and Dwayne was on the wing. Frank Dobbs was a great performer, too.

Our greatest weapon going into the tournaments in my senior year was that we were seasoned. That means a lot to kids that age. The fans don't realize how much. I came here as a freshman and fit into a successful program with a great team. We made the NCAA Tournament and I played in it. I know I took all that for granted. As you mature, you learn that you can't take things like that for granted. Only 64 teams in the whole country participate and you've got to earn your way into that pack. Once you do all that, only one team wins. You may only get one real good shot in four years. Well, Gary, Dwayne, and I had been there three other times. Now it was senior year. We knew exactly what that meant. We saw the Pinones and Grangers bow out without having done it. Teams with freshmen and sophomores don't have that sense of urgency and understanding. That only comes from experience and maturity.

1984-1985 Big East Standings

	THE BIG EAST			OVERALL		
	W-L	PCT	GB	W-L	PCT	NCAA
1. St. John's	15-1	.937	-	31-4	.886	3rd
2. Georgetown	14-2	.875	1	34-3	.919	2nd
3. Villanova	9-7	.563	6	25-10	.714	1st
4. Syracuse	9-7	.563	6	22-9	.710	
5. Pittsburgh	8-8	.500	7	17-12	.586	
6. Boston College	7-9	.438	8	20-11	.645	
7. Connecticut	6-10	.375	9	13-15	.464	
8. Providence	3-13	.188	12	11-20	.355	
9. Seton Hall	1-15	.063	14	10-18	.357	

The 'Cats had five days to lick their wounds after the Pittsburgh pummeling before once again entering the melee known as the Big East Tournament. 'Nova finished the season tied for third in the Big East with Syracuse. The Orangemen won a coin toss for the number-three seed. Thus, five days after Pittsburgh embarrassed them in front of a nationwide TV audience, the 'Cats had to face the Panthers again.

Villanova played tentatively at the start, dropping behind 21-13. The three seniors all stepped up to bring the 'Cats back.

STEVE PINONE: "Ed made the play of the season against Pittsburgh's Joey David. We had come out slow in that second Pittsburgh game. We could have folded, but it was obvious that the starters, and particularly the seniors, were out to prove something to Rollie. See? His strategy worked. Joey David got the ball at the foul line driving for a sure layup. Eddie was back at half court and he just ran upcourt, overtook David, and blocked the shot. Then Eddie hustled downcourt to jam in a followup and cut the lead to 21-17. I think that was the greatest individual effort I saw all year on any team. It showed we came to play and fired everyone up."

MARK PLANSKY: "To me, that play was key. For Ed to make that effort, to chase that guy down and turn it into, in effect, a four-point play, made a statement that picked up our whole team. Just days before, our attitude and effort were in question, and here comes Ed putting everything he had into that play."

Tear Drops

Ed Pinckney excelled at blocking shots. He ranks third on the 'Nova all-time list. One statistic that is not kept is how often those little penetrating guards *don't* get their shots blocked—the Alan Iversons and Jameer Nelsons of the world. Behemoths like E-Z Ed get frustrated or dazzled by certain guys time and again—guys who penetrate, tempt fate, and avert annihilation as deftly as Riki Tiki Tavi avoided a cobra's strike.

There were three little guards that I could never block: Reggie Theus, Sleepy Floyd at Georgetown, and Dan Callendrillo at Seton Hall. Some little guys just have the knack. Others never get it down. The great guys just float up a little teardrop that you can't get your hand on, and it floats down and goes in. When we practiced at Sacramento, Reggie used to taunt me, "You're never gonna get me!" I was determined to prove him wrong, but he was right. I never caught up with him.

Big East Tournament

D-Train shined as well in the Pitt rematch. Held scoreless till 49 seconds remained in the half, he suddenly came alive with a spectacular dunk followed by a free throw. Dwayne scored four more before the half ticked into history with Gary McLain's launching of a 45-footer that knotted the contest at 30.

Harold Pressley, who led all scorers and rebounders with 19 and 13 respectively, pushed the Wildcats ahead for good with 15:04 left in the second half. The 'Cats never looked back, rolling the lead up to double figures for much of the balance of the game. The final was 69-61, Villanova.

Villanova's semifinal opponent was St. John's. For the third time this season, the result was the same. Again, the trio

Harold Pressley emerged as a big star that championship season. (Photo courtesy of the Villanova Sports Information Department)

of Mullin-Berry-Wennington tallied 46. This time, two other members of the Red Force, Mike Moses (17) and Mike Jackson (10) added double figures to the tally.

St. John's jumped off to a nine-point advantage. Villanova stormed back to even it up, only to tail off and drag a six-point deficit into the locker room. Ed Pinkney tossed in a game-high 27 points along with five blocked shots and five rebounds, all for naught. 'Nova had hoped for a better showing to impress the NCAA tournament selection committee. Now they had to go back to the Main Line and sit anxiously through Selection Sunday. And hope.

Selection Sunday

We were all sitting in Coach Mass's office, convinced we should be picked. Sure we had ten losses, but half of them were to number-one and number-two teams. And they were close games. We knew we could play with anyone. Selection Sunday was always a fun time, a family time with Coach Mass. We sat in his office watching the CBS announcer. I think it was Gary Bender. We all shouted out when we were announced as the number-eight seed in the Southeast Regional. At that moment, we weren't worried about seeds, location, nothing. We were just happy to get the bid.

The bid to the NCAA Tournament was the Wildcats' sixth straight. That placed them in some pretty elite company. Arkansas, Georgetown, Kentucky, and North Carolina were the only other teams that could make the same boast.

It wasn't all good news for Villanova. Villanova would have to face number-nine seed Dayton on Dayton's home court. Dayton was 15-2 on that court.

Playing Dayton on their home court did not sit well with Coach Mass—not at all. He started calling people after that announcement, complaining, "Who ever heard of that? How can they play that game on their own court?" It didn't do any good, of course. But Rollie didn't like that situation at all.

On the positive side of the ledger, the news that there would be no shot clock in the tournament was welcomed by the patient Wildcats.

MARK PLANSKY: "I've heard that shot-clock thing discussed ever since we won the tournament. So many analysts felt that we wouldn't have won with a shot clock. If you look at the statistics, I don't think we exceeded the clock limits any more than our opponents did. We might have exceeded the shot clock twice in the final game. But that's not the real measure. We were a disciplined team that knew how to exploit the shot clock. A lot of teams don't.

"The shot clock does a few things. It allows you to rest on the court. That was important. We had a thin bench, so anything that gave our starters a breather was an advantage. The other advantage of no shot clock is that the defense doesn't know when you're going to run a play. That enables a disciplined team like ours to hold out for a sure shot. With a shot clock, the defense knows you're going to start the play when you wind down to 15 seconds or so. So yes, all things considered, I think we would have won even with a shot clock."

Chapter Five

THE
NCAA TOURNAMENT

Dayton Falls al Dente

BOB VETTRONE, Philadelphia writer: "We had a big dinner before the Dayton game. Rollie ordered some kind of dish that was supposed to be done al dente. I have no idea what that means. But whatever they brought out, it wasn't what Rollie figured it was supposed to be. He complained to the waiter who argued that it was al dente. Rollie wouldn't hear it and was not about to give in. Finally the chef came out, and told Rollie he was right. The chef then prepared a real al dente preparation and brought it out to Rollie."

Note to the gastronomically challenged: Al dente (literally, "to the teeth") is s a term used to describe pasta or food which is cooked until it offers only slight resistance when bitten into, and which is not soft or overdone.

Off to Dayton

Off they went into the wild blue yonder. Villanova winged out to Dayton to face a team they knew very little about. The 'Nova crowd was confident. After all, no Massimino-coached Villanova team ever lost a first-round NCAA playoff game. At that point, Rollie was 7-0 in first-round NCAA Tournament games. But the analysts and the anxious hastened to point out that this time it was different. Rollie and his boys were facing a tough team on its home hardwoods.

Rollie was beside himself when we drew Dayton. "This is unprecedented," he was ranting. "No team ever gets a home-court advantage in the NCAAs. We've got to show that selection committee they made a big mistake giving us that number-eight seed. We're better than that."

CRAIG MILLER: "Actually Rollie was a master at not letting things like that become distractions. He turned that whole Dayton home-court-advantage thing completely around in one day. He convinced our guys that Dayton was the visiting team, not us. His logic was flawless: 'We're seeded higher than they are. That makes us the home team in this game. Doesn't matter where they play it. We're the ones sitting on the home bench.'"

The experts anticipated a defensive marathon. They weren't disappointed. In a seesaw battle, the teams exchanged the first-half lead eight times. At the midpoint, the 'Cats trailed 23-21. That was a familiar feeling. They waited till the tournament final to lead at halftime.

This tilt went right down to the wire. Defense ruled. Late in the game, as Villanova clung to a 47-43 lead, Dayton strung six straight points together to inch ahead. Then Ed Pinckney hit a layup that knotted the score. On Dayton's next possession, Harold Pressley stole the ball from Anthony Grant. Summoning the great poise and confidence that became their hallmark, the 'Cats spread the floor with 2:30 remaining. Seventy-nine ticks later, Harold Jensen sprinted in for a virtually uncontested layup that put his team ahead.

Next it was Dayton's turn to hold the ball. With ten seconds to go, Dayton lofted a 17-foot jumper that missed the mark. Dayton got the rebound, however. Dayton's Sedric Toney gunned a 16-footer that failed. Big Ed Pinckney grabbed it off the boards and was immediately fouled. E-Z Ed missed the free throw but time ran out and it was a V for Villanova.

Villanova's patience, discipline, and experience determined the outcome. In typical fashion, they traded flash for substance. They concentrated on D—on handcuffing and frustrating their Midwest opponent rather than playing for points. E-Z Ed restricted center Dave Colbert to five points, a staggering 12.1 points below his seasonal average. And as they would do all Tournament, the Wildcats rose to the occasion. After shooting only 37.5 percent in the first half, they took a more disciplined, workmanlike approach that hiked their shooting percentage for the game all the way up to 47.6 percent.

Dayton was tough. Looking back, that was probably our toughest game in the whole tournament. We knew what to expect from Georgetown and St. John's. I think that causes less anxiety, even when they're considered the best teams in the nation. But Dayton was the great unknown to us, and that's always a little scary. Then when we played the game, we seemed to be playing real well, but not winning. We were playing and playing, and not pulling away from them. They were well coached and tough.

RON WILSON ("STATS"): "Harold Jensen emerged in that game. He couldn't have picked a better time. Harold hadn't played much, and hadn't played well for most of the season. But for some reason, I remember Dwight (Wilbur) telling me he was having a tough time playing on that surface in Dayton. He kind of psyched himself out about it. Then when Harold had a chance to come in for him, Harold brought his A game. When he hit that lay-up at Dayton, it gave him the confidence he had been lacking all season. Harold became a different player, at least in my eyes, from that moment on."

HARRY BOOTH, volunteer coach: "Rollie was simply a master psychologist. Not long before the Big East Tournament, Harold Jensen went to Rollie and questioned whether he should even be a Division I player. Harold had struggled with his confidence all season long. Rollie told him he wanted Harold to look for a good shot and start taking it. That talk did wonders for Harold."

Johnny Morris Joins the Family

ROB WILSON ("STATS"): "I don't think we can underestimate the effect Jake had on that team. The guys on the team, especially the seniors, had seen Jake fail terribly. He grew weaker and weaker each year. He was literally failing in front of their eyes. Jake Nevin was completely incapable of taking care of himself by the time the tournament came around. That's when Johnny Morris, Jake's nephew, started traveling everywhere with the team just to take care of Jake. Johnny was accepted as part of the family. Rollie was so good to him. He loved the man, and wanted so much to win it for him. So did the guys on the team. That was the ritual. They'd kiss Jake's head for good luck before each game."

Michigan

The Michigan match marked the sixth time that season that Villanova squared off against a number-one or number-two ranked team. Michigan had just unseated St. John's from the number-two slot. It was the first time all year that St. John's didn't occupy one of the top two positions in the polls.

Everyone on the team knew we'd beat Michigan. We kept telling each other, "We play Georgetown and St. John's. They don't." The guys on Michigan were mostly freshmen and sophomores. I think our guys—particularly the seniors—were kind of indignant about that—that they were so young and favored over a veteran team like ours. Michigan was athletic. They wanted to get up and down the court fast and play a fast-paced game. But we were feeling like, "You guys are underclassmen. We're not going to let you dictate the pace of this game." We didn't feel they could apply the kind of pressure Georgetown does. We were determined to execute properly and we did. That game was almost like fun. We were confident. We didn't feel pressure at all.

ROB WILSON ("STATS"): "The Michigan game was another game we wanted for Jake. We played it on March 17, St. Patty's Day—one of Jake's biggest days, of course. The guys had a lot of fun with winning that one for Jake."

Villanova recorded a 59-55 upset by holding Michigan to its lowest point production of the season. The 'Cats took a 30-26 lead into the locker room—which turned out to be the only game in the tournament they led at the half except against Georgetown. Villanova started the second half flat and dropped behind by five. 'Nova recaptured the lead with 3:26 remaining and was never again overtaken.

Michigan coach Billl Freider in his postgame comments remarked, "Villanova doesn't look like a team that lost ten games! They played a near-perfect game out there … it was the best game played against us (all year). Their execution was excellent. We made them take perimeter shots, but they hit them. We put them at the free-throw line and they hit them. I think their experience, six straight years in the tournament, helped. Veteran clubs are the ones that survive."

On to Birmingham: The Maryland Game

The 'Cats headed down to Birmingham Alabama to compete in the Southeast Regionals. Their victory over Michigan thrust them into the Sweet Sixteen. Their first-round opponent was Maryland, another highly touted team that had beaten them earlier in the year. Len Bias, who was selected ACC Player of the Year, had netted a career-high 30 in the first contest. Relentless defense won the game for the 'Cats who shot an uncharacteristic 36.9 percent from the floor and 66.7 percent from the foul line. The 'Cats handcuffed Bias.

MARTY MARBACH, Villanova coach on the '84-'85 squad: "That game was the only time in Bias's college career that he was held below 10. Ed Pinckney was unbelievable. All the guys were, but Eddie more than anyone."

Maryland held on to a one-point lead after one half, but started the second half ice cold. Villanova ran the lead up to as many as 10 but uncharacteristically squandered it when they went into their stall-ball mode. Maryland managed to close to within three at 43-40. Then Pinckney came up big, grabbing a couple of rebounds and knocking in a pair of free throws to seal the Wildcat win. The victory gave Rollie's quintet a ticket to the tournament's Elite Eight.

Against Maryland in that game, we played completely different than we did in the regular-season loss. We dictated the tempo of the game. That was so important to our success in the tournament. We took charge and made everyone play our game, And Coach Mass had us so disciplined, we wouldn't come down off that. Against Maryland, I think our coaches got us the win. They had us changing defenses constantly. We'd go from man to zone and then back to man again—then we'd go from full press to 3/4 press and back to zone. Maryland never knew what they were facing, and they never got themselves untracked. They were confused the whole game. And we were having fun the whole time. It loosened us up. Coach was big on that. He felt that tournament time was a time to enjoy and remember. It was the time to capitalize on everything you already learned.

The Pasta Bowl

What the hell was happening? The 'Cats were up against stiff competition, the seventh-ranked North Carolina Tar Heels. The Wildcats faced stiff competition all year long, but inexplicably Villanova was sleepwalking. They were practically lifeless for the first 20 minutes—shooting a putrid 23.1 percent from the field and 55.6 percent from the line, while managing only 17 points.

ROB WILSON ("STATS"): "We were down eight near the end of the half, then Dwayne got a tip-in with one second left. He was fouled and sank the free throw to cut NC's lead to five. We were flat and tight. That was the game Rollie made his legendary 'pasta speech.'

"Rollie usually got together with the coaches, talked things over, got his staff on the same page, then gathered the team and spoke to them. He didn't do that this game. He went right in, gathered the boys around him and started talking about pasta— yeah, pasta. He said something like, 'Do you really think I'd rather be here and not enjoying myself instead of sitting home relaxing, eating a big bowl of linguini with clams?' The guys were looking at one another trying to figure out what he was talking about! Soon it started to sink in. He was telling them to enjoy the moment. They were playing so tight they were ineffective. They weren't doing the things that brought them this far. They were throwing everything away—a great season, a great opportunity—and they weren't having a very good time in the process. It was really effective. They were a different team that second half. They made the most dramatic turnaround I ever saw."

Harold Jensen started in the second half for the first time. First thing he did was miss an 18-footer. North Carolina, however, turned the ball over, and Jensen reprised his shot successfully as the NC lead slimmed to three. Eight minutes into the half, 'Nova had jumped to a five-point lead. Despite an NC run that narrowed the gap to one, Villanova slowly took control of the lead, the tempo, and the contest. The 'Cat attack was balanced and deadly. Four guys—Pressley (15), McClain (11), McLain (11), and Jensen (10)—reached double figures, with Pinckney adding nine to the cause. In the second half, Villanova provided a harbinger of things to come, gunning a torrid 76.2 percent from the floor and 87.5 percent from the line.

MARK PLANSKY: "Dwight Wilbur was a great guard, but Harold Jensen got hot at the right time. Most people think Harold was the number-two guard that year. He wasn't. Dwight started every game. But it was a tribute to the togetherness and cohesion of our team and the coaching staff that Harold broke into the lineup when he got hot like that, and there was no dissension. The whole thing was kind of unspoken, just understood. Throughout the tournament, Dwight was still the starter. It's just that everyone knew Harold would go in as soon as the opportunity presented itself, and then he'd stay in."

Looking back, we were confident against North Carolina. Rollie told us not to read the papers. The writers didn't give us a chance. But we didn't believe any of it! Once again, we figured that we play in the Big East. We played tough teams all year long. Our schedule never gave us a break. We'd play the top two teams in the country back to back, then come back and play St. Joe's or Temple in the Big Five, and they'd want to kill us. Rollie's talk helped. We went out there in the second half and had fun.

Sports Illustrated Cover Pre-Jinx

There's a jinx attached to being on the cover of *Sports Illustrated*. The jinx goes something like this: if you make the cover, whatever had been going good will start going bad. It didn't work against the contrarians at Villanova. They continued their March march. But their cover guy for the shot, well, that's a different story.

When we had control of that NC game, Dwayne went in for a backwards dunk. That was my signature dunk, and Dwayne hadn't done one yet on our chart. I think he was waiting for the right moment, and this seemed like the right one. Well, he missed. When he landed, he started acting like his leg hurt. I'm thinking, "Get up, Dwayne. You are faking it. You're not hurt. You're just embarrassed." Turns out they put that dunk on the Sports Illustrated *cover—the dunk Dwayne missed. I couldn't believe it. D-Train was running around campus all week showing everybody the cover—and he missed the shot.*

Beating the Tar Heels

HAROLD JENSEN: "I got 10 points in the second half. My dad ran down to the floor and they were telling him he wasn't allowed on the court. He insisted, 'Let me by. I'm gonna hug my son!' which is just what he did. I got the MVP for the game and he was so proud. I'll never forget that moment."

CRAIG MILLER: "When we beat NC, we suddenly became the darlings of Philadelphia. You know when Philly gets behind you, there's nothing like it. No one had paid attention to us up to that game. But once we made the Final Four, everything changed. We had all the elements that made the city love us. Everyone figured we were overachieving. Philly

Harold "Norm" Jensen drives. Jensen's 10 points in the second half earned him game MVP against North Carolina. (Photo courtesy of the Villanova Sports Information Department)

loves overachievers and underdogs. We had a charismatic coach who wasn't neat and tidy, but who was emotional and wore his heart on his sleeve. And we did things our way. We didn't win pretty, but we won through persistence and guts. I'll tell you this. I learned so much watching Rollie through all this. He was a wise man. I remember getting carried away, saying to him, 'Everybody loves us now, Coach.' Rollie corrected me, 'No, everyone doesn't love us. There's nobody that everybody loves. There are people out there that would give anything to see us fail too.'"

CHUCK EVERSON: "When we got back to campus at about one a.m. after beating North Carolina, it was unreal. The whole school and fans from everywhere gathered to party at the gym all day waiting for the team to get back to campus. That gym was jam-packed. People were screaming. I felt like Ringo Starr with the Beatles. The big stars like Ed and Dwayne, were the reason we were winning. Those guys were like John Lennon and Paul McCartney. I was like Ringo. I was in the background as far as the team's success was concerned. But everyone, the whole team, was up there on the stage together, like we were all equal. Eddie never acted like a 'star.' He never considered himself any different, and certainly never considered himself better than anyone.

"While we were all on stage, we broke into 'My Girl.' The whole gym was singing along with us. That had sort of become our team's song. I don't know why. It was just one of those silly things. Steve Lappas used to sing it—well, he had to sing it. That was his first year at Villanova and that was Rollie's initiation ceremony. He made the new guys get up and sing. Whenever we had a dull moment or a tense moment or a fun moment, Rollie would make Steve stand up and sing it. After a while, the whole team got into it. It kind of became the song for that season."

When we got back from Birmingham, Villanova was crazed. I never saw anything like it. Every day, the gym was packed full for practices. All kinds of former players were showing up on campus. The atmosphere was unreal. I really felt we couldn't miss. I think the whole team felt that way.

Jake Nevin used to joke with us. One of his favorite pranks was to zap you with this canister of ice he carried with him. That was fun—loose and fun. But now Jake's health was too poor. He couldn't cut up at practices anymore. Jake was in bad shape. The stands were full. Things seemed different. I kind of wanted the old way back. And life on campus was crazy. I'd go back to my room and my door would be completely covered with notes and signs, "Go

Ed. Go 'Cats!" I'd take them down and go get something to eat, and when I'd come back, the door would be full of signs again.

The Final Four
God, I Hope We Win

The 1985 NCAA finals held a little more intrigue—well, in all honesty, a lot more intrigue—in terms of bragging rights. It's not unusual to pray for victory. But three of the four teams in the '85 final four sort of specialized in prayers. Three of four were Catholic schools. It's unlikely that will ever happen again. And although it might sound harmonious, the situation fostered a bit more rivalry than the norm.

Each school is administered by a different order of priests. Villanova is an Augustinian school, Georgetown a Vincentian school, and St. John's of New York a Jesuit school.

Let's liken the rivalry to brother versus brother in a wrestling tourney. Each brother is rooting for the other to finish second. Or maybe a better example would be Philadelphia's traditional Army vs. Navy game. Each team plays a little harder that game, even though—actually because—both serve the same commander in chief.

On the campus of St. John's at the time, there was a joke—maybe more of a hope—that went like this.

The Presidents at Villanova, St. John's and Georgetown signed, sealed, and sent a joint letter to God beseeching Him to let the best teaching order among the three win. God's reply came back: "I love each order equally. All excel, but I must remain impartial and show no favoritism."

The letter was signed: "God, SJ"

Note to non-Catholics: "SJ" stands for "Society of Jesus," commonly known as the Jesuits.

Memphis State

The Wildcats were off to Lexington, Kentucky, to play a pair of games.

When we were all in Lexington, even my mom was telling me, "You can be proud to get this far even if you don't win another game." I told her, "Mom, we're going to win this whole thing. We're not happy just to get this far. We're here to play two more games, and we're only going to be happy if we win both of them."

ROB WILSON ("STATS"): "Chuck Everson was the big music guy. On bus trips, Chuck always had the earphones on, listening to tapes. He was a big Phil Collins fan, and kept on singing 'One More Night' during the tournament. That kind of set the tone as we advanced. We took each game one at a time—just one more night, give us just one more night."

MARK PLANSKY: "That 'One More Night' theme you mentioned about Chuck was a real theme, I think. Rollie did a fabulous job of keeping us focused on the next game only. That's the only way to get through that tournament, and that's how he got us through so successfully, one game at a time."

ROB WILSON ("STATS"): "Lexington was our final location. That meant one final, quick suit cleaning for the team managers. We had to wear our 'lucky suits' each and every game during the NCAA Tournament. Whatever suit we wore the first night, we'd have to wear every other game. Coach Mass wore two suits. He wore the same suit for games one and two. The managers only had one suit. For us, it meant a mad rush to the dry cleaner in every city we were playing in. We'd rush our suits to the dry cleaners after we won, and rush back on game day to pick them up."

The Wildcats now had to face number-five ranked Memphis State. At this point, 'Nova had perfected its deliberate game. Linked to stingy defense, the slower tempo that the 'Cats set frustrated the Tigers at both ends of the court. Again, Villanova slowly took control as the game wore on.

The first half ended deadlocked. With 15:31 game minutes left, Villanova edged out 32-31 on Ed Pinckney's foul shots. Memphis State's two big men, 6'11" Keith Lee and 7'0" William Bedford played the remainder of the game in foul trouble. Lee eventually fouled out, along with Holmes. Memphis State thundered back to knot the score at 41, but from there on, it was all Villanova.

Villanova's stifling defense had choked the Tigers back to 45 points—their lowest tally of the year—29 points below their average. In fact, 'Nova was forcing their tournament opponents to shoot only 41 percent in averaging only 48 points.

After the contest, Memphis State coach Dana Kirk articulated the most pertinent observation of the Wildcats thus far. When questioned whether Villanova was a "Cinderella team," Captain Kirk replied: "If they're a Cinderella team, then Cinderella wears boots."

Rollie on the Road

VIC D'ASCENZO, senior team manager: "Rollie and the team were having a great time, making the most out of the whole experience. They were a diverse bunch and really got along well, cutting up with each other and having fun. They were always riding somebody for something. Like Connally Brown. Connally came from Texas and was always freezing. He used to keep his hotel room like a furnace, so the northern guys never let him up about being a wuss."

HAROLD JENSEN: "We were like a family when we were on the road. After practice, Rollie would take us back to the hotel. We'd go to his room, eat great, and sit around and watch a tape of the next team. Rollie would test us on the scouting reports. He made the postseason fun."

The Villanova team and their "family" pose in front of the Ramada in Lexington. (Photo courtesy of the Villanova Sports Information Department)

CHUCK EVERSON: "I've never been on a team that was so close. We did everything together—go to dinner, movies, everything. And there was always a bunch of us—not just three or four, and not the same guys all the time, either. We all got along.

"And I agree with Vic. We were always on somebody's case. Gary was the funniest guy. He'd always have his mouth going—kept the bus trips lively. And Wyatt and me were his biggest targets, literally and otherwise. We'd pass by a train station and depot, and Gary would yell up to us, 'Chuck, didn't I tell you to put your trains away before you went to bed!'"

VIC D'ASCENZO: "When we were on the road, we'd eat our meals together. We'd have fun and cut loose. But we had mass together too. Father Lazor, the team chaplain, used to say mass either in his room or Rollie's."

Rollie Massimino and his team relax and visit a horse farm in Lexington at the Final Four. (Photo courtesy of the Villanova Sports Information Department)

To the Nines

JIM DELORENZO, former Villanova sports information director: "Lucky suits weren't our only superstition. We had this thing going with the number nine. Father Lazor, the chaplain who's still at Villanova started it. He'd come into the sports information office before every game and ask for nine programs. Why nine? I don't know. We never asked. Anyway, our basketball manager that year, Rob Wilson (Stats), made it kind of 'a thing.' Stats would always run around holding up nine fingers. Hey that's better than one, isn't it? Anyway, someone picked up on the fact that Villanova has nine letters and we were playing for the national championship in Lexington, which has nine letters, and Father Lazor was going to be there, probably bugging someone for nine programs. We figured it all meant one thing: Villanova was going to win. Don't ask me how it added up to that, but you get superstitious as hell when you're on a roll like we were on that you can't explain."

Happy Meals

Ever wonder what teams are jawing about in their huddles during timeouts? Fans figure they're improvising brilliant strategy, or hearing a Rockneyesque motivational speech. Nah! That wasn't it.

I think one of our biggest motivators during the playoffs was meal money. We got $25 when we were on the road. You can't believe how that motivated us. We actually broke huddles by putting our hands together and shouting, "Meal Money!"

ROB WILSON ("STATS"): "Yeah, I handed out those brown envelopes. Ask any of the guys if they remember the brown envelopes. They will. That's what the meal money came in. The amount was graduated, depending on where we played and what part of the season it was. We got five dollars for snacks for a home game and eight dollars for a road game. Then the amount went up: $25 for a day on the road, $35 for a Big East Tournament game, and $50 a day for the NCAA Tournament. Nothing motivated those guys like meal money!"

Chapter Six

APRIL FOOL'S DAY

Championship Game
God Lives on the Main Line

Another joke was stoking the Catholic-school rivalry between Villanova's Augustinians and Georgetown's Vincentians as they prepped for the final leg of the NCAA Tournament. It went like this.

A sportswriter decided to visit the two campuses and interview the president of each school. First he went to Georgetown. After a pleasant conversation with Georgetown president Rev. Timothy Healy, SJ, he spotted a golden telephone in a special room filled with magnificent art and gilded curtains. He asked what it was, and Father Healy replied, "Oh that's a direct line to God. "When the good Father offered him the chance to place a call, the sportswriter was thrilled 'till Father Healy told him, 'It costs $100,000 a minute.'" (Note to non-sportswriters: that price is approximately $99,999.90 a minute beyond any sportswriter's budget). Disappointed, the writer declined.

Next, the writer visited Villanova. When he and Villanova President Reverend John M. Driscoll bustled down a modest hallway, they passed a little black plastic phone. Next to the phone was a piece of cardboard with "Direct Line to God" scrawled on it in magic marker. Father Driscoll asked, "Would you like to use it?" The sportswriter replied without hesitation, "I can't afford it." Father Driscoll looked puzzled: "You can't afford a quarter?" The sportswriter said, "A quarter! But it's $100,000 a minute at Georgetown! What's the big difference?" "Why," the good Father smiled, "That's because at Villanova, it's a local call."

Hoya Paranoia—Not

The line on the game was nine and a half points. To the outside world, Villanova didn't have a chance against NCAA defending champion Georgetown.

DWAYNE McCLAIN: "We had more than a chance. We always thought we would win if we could only get to that game. We felt that way for four years. We watched the NCAA final on TV our freshman year when Georgetown almost beat North Carolina. Remember? Fred Brown turned the ball over to James Worthy. Georgetown stayed right with those guys, and they had Worthy and Jordan. We realized early on that we were good enough to play with anyone. Besides, we played Georgetown at least twice every year. We always felt we could compete with them.

"When we got to the Final Four in '85, that wasn't fulfilling enough for me—or for Ed or Gary. We had competed in the tournament all four years, and we knew this year was our last chance. Now that we finally made the Final Four, we had our minds set on going all the way. We wouldn't have been satisfied with anything less."

In typical understated fashion, the 'Cats stayed in modest accommodations, a Ramada Inn in Lexington. In contrast, the Hoyas were sequestered miles away. Coach Mass seemed completely relaxed, just taking in the whole affair. He passed his joy on to his young charges, which did not go unnoticed by the press. In fact, what they witnessed at Villanova's open practice session bewildered fans and media alike.

CHUCK EVERSON: "We were enjoying the whole experience, following Coach Mass's lead. When we got to Lexington, we had a workout—there must have been 15,000 people in the stands. The arena was packed. St. John's, Memphis State, and Georgetown all went through a serious practice. Coach Mass told us, 'Look, I've taught you all I can at this point. If you don't have it by now, it's too late. You'll never get it. But you guys do get it, so let's have some fun.' The last 15 minutes of our practice, we split the squad up and played a pickup game. Actually we split up and played the African American guys versus the white guys. We had a great time! The spectators couldn't believe we were cutting up like that. But it was a terrific idea, and turned into a really effective practice session. It kept us loose and brought us even closer as a squad. To this day, we argue about who won that pick-up game! When you're talking to Eddie, tell him I said we schooled them!"

CRAIG MILLER (Villanova manager on the '84-'85 squad): "Yes, Rollie was loose. But don't get the idea he was on a lark. When Rollie told them to play that pickup game, that was one practice. He had another practice out there in Lexington. He managed to secure a high school gym so we could practice away from the public and press. That was a good practice session, too.

"Meanwhile, the crush for game tickets was on. Rollie wanted everyone in the Villanova family—I mean everyone—at that game. And people started crawling out of the woodwork asking for tickets.

"Rollie invited Al Severance and all the former players, everyone who ever participated in the Villanova program. Rollie was wholeheartedly devoted to the notion of family. This team was family to him, and the Villanova community, past and present, was extended family. Rollie was like a dad who can't have a nice Christmas unless all his kids come back."

Going into the contest, Villanova had more than enough emotional incentive. If ever trainer Jake Nevin were to see a Wildcat national champ, this had to be the year. Then unexpectedly, tragedy struck the morning of the game.

BOB VETRONE: "I was rooming with Al. At 7 a.m. on Monday morning, I left the room and went downstairs to do a show on WCAU, radio1210 in Philly. Afterwards, I went to the coffee shop. When I got back to the room, Al was lying dead in the middle of the room. Apparently, he showered and shaved and then had a fatal heart attack. I telephoned Ted Aceto. Ted took care of everything from that point on. I was scheduled to broadcast the game that night, but I was too shaken to go on. Whitey Rigsby (former Wildcat player and longtime announcer) took my place. I sat in the stands and watched the game with Mike Mulquin and Joe Rogers (ex-Villanova players).

CRAIG MILLER: "It was so strange that day with Al Severance dying. I think our breakfast that morning came from a vending machine at the Ramada where we were staying."

Take the Tickets and Run

JIM DELORENZO: "People didn't believe we were gonna do it that year. We didn't hear anything from the Philadelphia media all season long, until we made the Final Four. Then the floodgates opened! Our ticket person, Lee Donar, was swamped, so, as resident jack of all trades, I jumped in to help. I rode down to the Philadelphia airport and picked up our insured package of 2,000 tickets. Everyone wanted a ticket, and Rollie—God bless him—was trying to get a ticket into everyone's hands. We had 4,000 to 6,000 requests—just in the period of a day or two. There I was, sitting on the floor of our office at two in the morning with piles of tickets and long lists of names, trying to sort everything out and beat the clock. I was a 22-year-old kid at the time, making all of $300 a month as the graduate assistant to the athletic director, Ted Aceto. It suddenly occurred to me, "I'm sitting on a gold mine! Two thousand tickets—how much could I get for these?"

"I don't know whether I changed my mind because of Catholic school training, a guilty conscience, fear—or that I had a really slow getaway car, but I didn't give into the temptation. When the smoke cleared, I was the only one I can even think of who did *not* get a ticket, and I was the one doling them out!"

If every man has his price, Jim, you can substantiate that yours exceeds $200,000—that's 2,000 tickets at an average of $100 a ticket. Of course, had you taken it and invested it all in dot-coms, you could have become 'Nova's biggest benefactor—and that's after treating yourself to a fast getaway car.

They Also Serve Who Stay at Home and (Gain) Weight

JIM DELORENZO: "It was a dirty job, and I was the one who had to do it. I stayed back. Everyone (else) was out in Lexington for the championship game. I can't blame Rollie. He did want me to go to the game. When I told him I couldn't go, he got fired up. Did you know Rollie could get fired up? He was yelling: 'That's not right!' But I was low man on the totem pole. Even more important, Villanova's baseball team had a doubleheader that Saturday and another game on Sunday. Believe it or not, all three games were against Georgetown. It was the first season of Big East baseball and we were taking the games seriously (52 Villanovans have played major league baseball). We were also hosting a high school track meet and a lacrosse game. So I stayed back.

"Wanna know how I watched the final game? Sitting on the couch in Rollie's office eating pizza and answering phones. Can you believe people were actually calling for Rollie during the game? I told them, 'No, you can't speak to him right now. But you can see him. Turn on the TV. He's the short guy waving his arms.'"

Thinking Upset

Chuck Everson's "One More Night" was a good soundtrack for the tournament, although on April Fool's Day 1985, "I Can Feel It Coming In the Air Tonight" might have been a better choice. Georgetown scored two victories over Villanova that year, but they never pushed the 'Cats around. The national press seemed to overlook that history. The 'Cats were not feeling upset. They were thinking "upset."

Fear Factor

We knew the guys from Georgetown. They didn't intimidate us. We played Georgetown twice each season. To be honest, we thought no one could beat us. I think a lot of teams read about Patrick Ewing, David Wingate, and the rest, and they let themselves get beat before they got on the court. We watched all the Georgetown games on TV.

We got to know them well. We could tell from the way other teams reacted at the tipoff that they were intimidated. The way teams brought the ball up the court, the way their players moved without the ball—you can tell when a team is intimidated. But we knew Georgetown. I knew Patrick back when I was in high school. I met him at Five Star Camp. We beat Georgetown the year before, and we played Georgetown tough every game for four years. We always took the court believing we would win—not that we could win, but that we would win. Strangely, we probably were more afraid of Dayton. None of us knew any of those guys. I think fear of the unknown is worse.

I remember sitting around on Selection Sunday, hearing that we were playing Dayton. Once the happiness died down and we got a chance to think, the whole team was like, "We'll get cheated! We'll be in the Midwest, we'll have the refs against us, and how are we gonna get tickets?" We didn't have those fears against the Hoyas.

So that's the way the 22-year-old (more accurately, 22-year, six-day-old) Ed Pinckney viewed matters. How about today? Through the focusing prism of hindsight and sagacity, how would the older, wiser Ed Pinckney assess 'Nova's chances today?

I'd be afraid! I mean, you've got Patrick underneath, Michael Jackson can shoot, Reggie Williams can kill you on the left wing, and Billy Martin is a tough baseline guy. Those guys had weapons!

Getting Ready for Georgetown

We matched up well with Georgetown. I watched some of the Georgetown—St. John's game after we beat Memphis State, not the whole thing—just 'til I was sure Georgetown had control. There was always a point in a Georgetown game where they just had the other team beat. You could tell. Their pressure started to break an opponent down. Then it was all over. I figured Georgetown had the

St. John's game all wrapped up, so I left. But I left happy. What no one realizes is that we would rather have faced Georgetown than St. John's. We didn't match up well with St. John's. Basketball is always a game of match-ups, and I think St. John's had our number that year. I don't think we'd have beaten them.

DWAYNE McCLAIN: "We played Georgetown well. Rollie made us disciplined. The first game my senior year, we were running with them for about two minutes, playing a real fast-paced game. Rollie called timeout and told us, 'This isn't gonna work. You guys gotta slow it down. That's how we're gonna beat these guys.' So we did and, though we fell short that night, the strategy worked in the championship game. They had a little more talent than us. But they weren't going to beat us every time. If we played them a hundred times, they might beat us sixty, but we'd have a good number of wins too. We felt strong going into that game. Let me tell you, it's tough to beat a team three times in one year, but I agree with Eddie. When Georgetown won that game against St. John's after we beat Memphis State, I felt like Villanova was going to win! We didn't match up with St. John's as well as we did with Georgetown."

CHUCK EVERSON: "I disagree with Ed and D-Train. We were going to win that night, period. It didn't matter who we played. There was a feeling in the air that night."

ROB WILSON ("STATS"): "Nothing bothered our team. They liked that role of underdog. The day of the Georgetown game, the paper in Lexington ran an article that said: 'There will be a Martian in the White House before Villanova beats Georgetown in the Finals.'"

You can't believe everything you read. President Reagan's first comment after the game was not Klaatu Barata Niktu.

ROB WILSON ("STATS"): "Somehow it wound up that there were four priests at the team supper before the Georgetown game: Father Lazor, the team chaplain, Father Driscoll, the school president, Father Hastings, and one other priest that

I can't recall right now. The joke at the dinner was that each priest represented one of the four regions in the NCAA."

No Two Jakes

ROB WILSON ("STATS"): "It was great to have Jake at the tournament. He was fun on the road. He had a quip for every occasion. He'd sit at a restaurant, stare at the waitress's ear and ask: 'Why are you only wearing one earring?' Of course, she'd be wearing two, but she'd get all flustered, and check out her ears. When people would ask about his longevity as a trainer, 'How long have you been here?' Jake would always say the same thing, 'Since about eight this morning.'

"Jake saw a lot of the country traveling with Villanova teams all those years. He'd tell anyone who wanted to listen, 'I've been in every state but Alaska and pregnancy.' He'd be asked how he contracted Lou Gehrig's Disease, and he'd shoot back, 'I don't know. I don't even play baseball.'

"No Jake never changed, not even when he was sick. He was the same old Jake."

Winning Thoughts

HAROLD JENSEN: "Coach Mass was never overwhelmed by the pageantry. He always conveyed to us that we could win. In fact, what he did after Mass the day of the game was one of the most effective things I ever experienced. He told us that on a one-shot deal, we could beat anyone in the nation. Then he told us to go think about this, 'Play to win. Don't play not to lose.'"

Playing to Win

The Wildcats came to play. They dictated the pace and flow of the game. The Hoyas did not. History records 'Nova's victory as perhaps the greatest upset in the Tournament's storied history. More than an upset, it was a testament to what preparation, self-belief and discipline can accomplish when a talented, determined bunch refuse to be intimidated or compliant to a script written by others. Villanova let no man write their epitaph on April Fool's Day. Georgetown was the toughest defensive team in all of college basketball. Yet, when the final tallies were in, Villanova had dazzled the Hoyas with unerring 78.6-percent shooting from the field, and a dazzling 90-percent shooting percentage from the foul line.

VIC D'ASCENZO: "They called that game a 'perfect game.' In an interview the day before the game, Rollie mentioned it would take a perfect game for us to win. Well, if the guys played a perfect game, it was because Rollie and his staff had prepared for the Hoyas perfectly. They got their ideas across to the team perfectly. And then the guys executed perfectly.

"The coaches always scratched a number on the chalkboard in the locker room. That was the magic number. Hold the other team to that number and we win. You know what the number on the chalkboard for the Georgetown game was? It was 64."

The game started according to script. Georgetown jumped out to an early lead, which bloated to six a few times in the early going. But Villanova hung in. They never allowed the Georgetown shark, as Ed Pinckney described the Georgetown attack, to grab hold. As the half drew to a close, Pinckney was on the bench with two fouls. The 'Cats were playing for one final shot. Georgetown did not challenge them aggressively, and with four seconds left, Harold Pressley busted a move and missed. The alert Prez, however, followed up and his bucket sent the Wildcats into the locker room with a one-point lead.

Ed Pinckney's (left) tough defense was a key to the April Fool's Day upset. (Photo courtesy of the Villanova Sports Information Department)

As the buzzer sounded, there was an incident that fired up 'Nova and riled its fiery coach.

CHUCK EVERSON: "Oh, yeah, the fight! I'm glad it happened. It keeps my name alive! I get interviewed about it every year during March Madness. What happened was: I saw Reggie Williams breaking for the basket and went to box him out. He went down, got back up, and took a shot at me. I was screaming at the ref for a foul. That's all I wanted. I figured Ed would return the second half, and this would be my only chance to score in a national championship game! When we left the court—well, everyone has that frame frozen in their minds. Rollie's running off the court pumping his fist. What people don't know is that we had to cross the Georgetown guys in the hall on our way to the locker room. They were all laughing, and I think that fired us up more than anything. It was kind of a lack of respect thing."

HARRY BOOTH: "Rollie made a great point about that Williams's incident at halftime. He told the kids, 'That play proves they can't beat us. That's what they have to resort to to win. They will not break us.'"

We've Got Them Right Where We Want Them

Some teams can't stand prosperity. In the glory days of Tom Landry's Dallas dynasty, Jolly Roger Staubach was uncanny for his ability to snatch victory from the jaws of defeat just as the game clock expired. The Cowboys trailed at halftime in practically every game that year. So the 'Boys found no need to panic when they were in the hole at halftime in the Super Bowl. A confident Tom Landry assured his team at intermission, "We've got them right where we want them."

Maybe that's where Villanova should have wanted to be—trailing at halftime. 'Nova *led* at halftime in every '84-'85 Big East battle against archrivals Georgetown and St. John's but one (the loss to St. John's in the Big East Tournament), and ended up losing.

MARK PLANSKY: "I attribute those halftime leads to Rollie Massimino's coaching ability. He and his staff prepared so well that we typically got the early jump on the other team. But I also believe Georgetown and St. John's were more talented, and after the first half, they'd catch us by virtue of their talent."

The Final 20 Minutes

The second half opened with a go-ahead bucket by Patrick Ewing. Jensen answered with a 16-footer. Then after Pinckney intercepted a pass, he dropped a bucket and foul shot at the other end of the floor, putting the 'Cats ahead by four. The lead swelled to six on a McLain jumper. The Hoyas, however, scratched back to regain the lead with less than four minutes remaining. The Wildcats coolly held the ball, looking for a good shot. Jensen selected a sure shot and didn't miss. His 16-footer with 2:36 remaining put the 'Cats ahead to stay. Still, a little more agita awaited Rollie and his boys.

Twice 'Nova missed the front end of one-and-ones with less than 1:10 to go and a five-point lead. Sinking either would have iced the game. As it was, the 'Cats' 61-56 advantage shrunk to three on a Ewing slam. Gary McLain answered, sinking four consecutive tries from the charity stripe. With the lead now at 65-61, the 'Cats conceded a Hoyas' layup. With ten ticks to go, Prez went to the foul stripe, and sank one of two for a 66-62 Villanova edge. Georgetown drove downcourt madly for a layup, narrowing the gap to two. Jensen inbounded

Ed Pinckney (left) and Gary McLain hang on in a tight Georgetown thriller. (Photo courtesy of the Villanova Sports Information Department)

to D-Train who had tripped but clutched the ball securely while lying on the hardwood awaiting the buzzer.

DWAYNE McCLAIN: "I was going crazy down there on the floor waiting for that buzzer. If you watch the tape, you can hear me yelling, 'Norm, Norm (Dwayne had pinned the nickname "Norm" on Harold Jensen).' I wanted to make sure he was clear if I had to toss the ball to him.'"

Gary McLain looks back as victory appears imminent with Villanova ahead 62-58 and 39 seconds left. (Photo courtesy of the Villanova Sports Information Department)

HARRY BOOTH: "I can still hear Ed yelling over and over, 'Can you believe this?' and Dwayne yelling, 'Yeah, April Fool!'"

In the eyes of the nation, David had beaten Goliath. Villanova pulled off the impossible dream by playing a "perfect game."

More than anything, Gary McLain made the difference. Georgetown beat everyone into submission with their press. We just got more and more confident as the game wore on because Gary was beating their press time after time. And the way we shot! I think our accuracy came from knowing that Gary was going to get the ball upcourt every time. Beating that press elevated every aspect of our play. I can still remember that feeling, positioning myself for offensive rebounds. Time after time, I'm working for position and watching shots swish through the net. We got into such a powerful rhythm. I just knew we were going to win.

HARRY BOOTH: "Success in the NCAA Tournament starts with a point guard. You can't win without a good one, and Gary was great. Georgetown had great guards, but you could see from the beginning, they didn't faze Gary at all. He actually had a smile on his face bringing the ball up. It was like he was saying, 'This is my game. This is my night, and you can't stop me.'"

ROB WILSON ("STATS"): "Rollie was giddy after the game. He was so happy for his 'family'—so proud. And to win for Jake, and win after the Al Severance shocker that morning. I can hear him yet in the postgame interview saying, 'Al Severance was up there in heaven swatting balls away for Villanova.' Rollie just might have been on to something there."

For D-Train, the game was sweet revenge of an old high-school debt.

DWAYNE McCLAIN: "In my senior year in high school, my team lost to Patrick Ewing's team in the state finals. Paul Cormier was recruiting me for Villanova. He watched the game, and signed something in my yearbook like, 'We'll get Patrick back later.' I showed it to Patrick after the high-school championship. Well, you know what—the first thing I did after the Georgetown game was to run over to Patrick. He knew what was coming. I said, 'I told you I'd get you back, Patrick!'"

ROB WILSON ("STATS"): "The whole team sang 'We Are the Champions'" on the bus coming back from the arena to the hotel. When we got to the hotel—the Ramada—the parking lot was so full, we couldn't get in. St. John's was staying

Gary McLain, John Pinone, Harold Pressley, and Ed Pinckney celebrate after a win over Georgetown. (Photo courtesy of the Villanova Sports Information Department)

across the way from us at another hotel. The Ramada only had two floors. Every square inch was filled with people, inside and out. We had an early flight the next morning but not a soul slept that night."

CRAIG MILLER: "I was the assistant SID, but the press didn't bother with Villanova that week! Nobody thought Villanova had a chance to win. Only one media person—a woman from *Good Morning America*—approached me. She asked if Villanova would arrange for some of our players to appear on the show if we won. She was just covering her bases—asking 'just in case.' But she was the only one from the national media who even bothered us all week. That's how Ed wound up on *Good Morning America*."

MARK PLANSKY: "When we got back to the hotel after that game, it was like a rock concert mob scene. That was the last I saw of Coach Mass till the next morning when we flew home. Coach stood in the bus when we finally got into the parking lot and told us, 'Enjoy the evening. You earned it. Have a great time and I'll see you tomorrow on the plane.'"

Who? Me?

MARK PLANSKY: "Oh I got into that game all right. I didn't expect to, and I went in when I least expected to. Gary had gotten run over on one play and we had to shoot a technical. On the bench, we were doing our job—we immediately started to work Dwight Wilbur over, saying he's gonna shoot an airball in front of 22,000 people. I almost fell over when Harry Booth yelled, 'Plansky.' I couldn't get my shooting shirt off. I had cottonmouth, and next thing I know, I'm hustling into the game. All the coaches are yelling instructions, and I'm running onto the court to play in front of the world. I was on and off the court fast and didn't have a very good appearance. But Coach

Mass made it a point to come down to where I was sitting on the bench and say, 'Great job.' It meant the world to me."

Mark Plansky was the only freshman on the championship squad and went on to star for three more years. (Photo courtesy of the Villanova Sports Information Department)

TV and Records

Everyone wanted to watch David take on Goliath. The Georgetown-Villanova game was at the time the second highest rated televised college basketball game of all time with a 23.3 rating, which measures a 33 share. The March 26, 1979 Michigan State-Indiana State (Larry Byrd vs. Magic Johnson), had a 24.1 rating, and 38 share. Measured by the number of homes watching, Georgetown-Villanova ranked fourth with 19,780,000 homes tuned in. Tops of all time was the April 6, 1992 Duke - Michigan tilt.

Gary McLain and Chuck Everson raise the NCAA Championship trophy. (Photo courtesy of the Villanova Sports Information Department)

A few all-time records that will be difficult to break were set. Villanova's 28 field goals attempted were the fewest ever in a final, as were the 17 rebounds the 'Cats pulled down. Individually, Ed Pinckney topped everyone in the tournament with 48 rebounds in six games. Dwayne McClain led all free-throw shooters with a blazing 24-25, 96 percent accuracy.

The Aftermath

At approximately 11:07 p.m. on April Fool's Day, the Main Line, Ed Pinckney's playground for the past four years, let its hair down. Bars and restaurants overflowed up and down the Main Line. By midnight, traffic along Lancaster Pike, the main artery that skirts the Villanova campus, was paralyzed. A half-hour later, Radnor police shut it down.

American Graffiti on the Main Line

JIM DELORENZO: "What a night that was when we won the championship! One of my many duties—well, once we won, it became my main duty—was to handle 'security' at the Field House. Fifty state troopers were dispatched to campus to prevent any overexuberance or vandalism or whatever. I was the point man because the entire administration and a good portion of the student body were in Lexington.

"After the game ended late that night, that impromptu celebration kicked in. Everyone was cruising up and down Lancaster Avenue, honking horns and screaming. A friend of mine, Andy McGovern, and I headed to what we call Villanova's 'grassy knoll.' It's at Lancaster Avenue and Ithan

Road. Andy was the intramural director and former woman's basketball coach. Like me, poor Andy drew the short straw and had to stay back on campus.

"Anyway, Andy and I are sitting on the grassy knoll watching the circus out on the street. All of a sudden, this car whizzes by with a girl sitting on the hood screaming out, 'Jim! Jim! Wasn't that awesome!'

"Turns out it was my younger sister. She was a junior at Immaculata College, which is about 15-20 minutes away from Villanova."

"I thought, 'Isn't this great! Even my sister's out celebrating, and I'm stuck here protecting the Field House.' I'm proud to say that the Field House went untouched. There was some minor damage elsewhere, nothing big. I'm also proud to say that I've kept my word to my sister. She made me promise never to tell our parents she was out that night on the hood of a car."

Jim, tell your sister her secret is still safe.

Philadelphia Frenzy

In center city, all night long, PECO Energy's Tower of Lights blazed: "'Nova #1." In Lexington, the Wildcats and the Wildcat faithful partied all night long. At 9 a.m., the team and "family" boarded their chartered Ozark jet for the hour and a half flight to Philly International. The plane touched down on an early spring, windy, chilly Philly day, to the hoots and hollers of 300 well wishers. Philadelphia had swiftly thrown together a parade for its now favorite sons. The City of Brotherly Love had staged parades in the not too distant past for the 1983 NBA champion Philadelphia 76ers, and the 1984 USFL champions, the Philadelphia Stars.

High noon was the official parade start. Three flatbeds set out from 17th and JFK Boulevard. Cheerleaders and the band were crammed on the lead truck. Media and photographers piled into the second, while the team and coaches climbed aboard the third. Philadelphians turned out in droves.

I couldn't believe it. I never saw anything like it. I really grew to love Philly and the people here. They were awesome. I remember the construction workers we passed along the way. They were all yelling and flashing "We're Number One." Then there were all those people who climbed into the trees around the plaza. We were tired from no sleep, but the parade and turnout woke us up. It was awesome.

The flotilla stopped at JFK Plaza. Everyone disembarked and mounted a stage constructed for the occasion. Mayor Wilson Goode phoned from Pittsburgh and congratulated the team. Next, Villanova president Rev. John M. Driscoll, related how proud the entire Villanova community was. Ed Pinckney then ascended the podium as Philly rocked to the chant of: "Ed-die, Ed-die ..."

E-Z Ed left a legacy for Philadelphia's sport gallery—the image of an exuberant, youthful Ed Pinckney holding the NCAA championship trophy aloft. The Wildcats' beaming hero epitomized Villanova. The victors came across as a group of well behaved, likeable kids who beat the odds. In a big, bad world, the Villanovans strode the world stage with dignity and aplomb.

After E-Z Ed addressed the throng, Coach Mass roused the crowds into some big cheers for his charges. Villanova's proud father crowed, "On behalf of Villanova University, which I am so proud of, this win was not only for us as players and coaches and family, It was for Villanova University, and all of you people and especially for Philadelphia. Thank you very much."

ROB WILSON ("STATS"): "We were always afraid to mention it to Coach Mass, but on the platform in front of City Hall when he spoke he said, 'It's an honor and pleasure to be here with the national champs of the nation.' Craig Miller and I looked at each other and chuckled. We used to watch it on tape all the time and got a kick out of it. But we never mentioned it to Coach Mass."

The Curse of Billy Penn

As of this writing, Villanova holds the dubious distinction of inspiring Philly's last (but hopefully not final) victory parade. The Flyers of the mid-seventies ushered in an era of relative prosperity for the Quaker City. The Phillies, of course, staged a huge victory parade in 1980. The 1983 '76ers and the 1984 Philadelphia Stars also enjoyed big center-city bashes. However, since Villanova's 1985 NCAA championship parade, the Quaker City has had no excuse to celebrate. Many locals blame Billy Penn. The statue atop City Hall had always set the limit for the height of new buildings. One Liberty Place, the first Philadelphia building higher than Billy Penn's statue, was erected in 1985. Ever since it started beautifying the Quaker City skyline, no Philly team has won a championship. Some call it the "Curse of Billy Penn." To winner-starved Philadelphians, the curse is getting serious.

Another Rollie Original

JIM DELORENZO: "I didn't leave the Villanova campus until 4 a.m. after we beat Georgetown. I drove back to my King of Prussia apartment, slept an hour, and zipped back to Villanova again. Everyone was still down in Lexington. All the phones in the athletic offices were routed to one phone. I answered one call after another all day, nonstop. I hunkered down in Rollie's office with a pink pad writing all the information down. It wasn't an easy job ("Hi. I'm John Doe. I met Rollie 20 years ago while we were waiting for a train. Tell Rollie I said hi and send him my congratulations. Here's my number—yes, my name is Doe, John Doe. That's spelled Doe, D-o-u-g-h.")

"One of the calls was not annoying. The White House called to say that President Reagan wanted the team to come down to Washington the next day. When Rollie finally arrived, I told him about the invitation. He was so beat, he didn't even flinch. I just passed the note with the information on it to his secretary.

"Rollie was looking out for his kids. They were tired and still a bit in shock after the game. Everything was happening so fast. Most of them hadn't been back to campus or hadn't seen their families for a long while. So, Rollie ended up delaying the visit to the White House. That's not as unusual these days. But back then, everyone headed to the White House within a day or two of the championship. I noticed the Florida Marlins didn't go to the White House this year till February, but back then, that wasn't the case. As always, Rollie was an original."

Norm

Harold Jensen had been a high school legend in Connecticut. Highly recruited, he followed Ed Pinckney and Harold Pressley to Villanova.

HAROLD JENSEN: "I turned down UCLA, Syracuse, and South Carolina. I had watched John Pinone and Harold Pressley in high school. I had gone to the Big East Tournaments with my dad over the years. At Villanova, I just felt at home. The atmosphere was like family, even though Digger Phelps sent me a postcard from Europe when I was in high school! When all is said and done, Villanova was an easy choice.

But things didn't go the way Harold Jensen had hoped. He was having trouble. Freshman year was disappointing, and sophomore year was going the same way.

HARRY BOOTH: "Harold was having a bad crisis of confidence. He went to Rollie before the Big East Tournament his sophomore year, and told him he had doubts about whether he was a Division I player. Rollie told him to relax, enjoy the game, and start taking shots when he had them. He did turn things around."

Jensen's performance in the NCAA tournament his sophomore year assured him a spot forever in the Villanova galaxy of sport heroes. But Harold constantly had to battle his own intensity.

DWAYNE McCLAIN: "I named Harold Jensen 'Norm' for Norman Bates. He was scary. Norm would get that look in his eye like a psychotic. He scared me sometimes. Actually, Harold was just a different breed. He was so intelligent and intense that he operated at a different level."

CHUCK EVERSON: "I remember Harold running through plays himself. He'd bounce the ball high in the air and run to where the second guy in the play would be. Then he'd bounce it to the third guy. Was he doing it for real or to amuse us? I hope he was doing it to be funny!"

HAROLD JENSEN: "School was tough when I first got there. I had to master time management. We had mandatory study hall every night for three hours after practice. Once you got a certain grade, study hall was optional from sophomore year on. It was mandatory for freshmen no matter what. But life was regimented. We had 2 p.m. practice, then we'd go to Dougherty Hall to eat, and then back down to the basketball offices to study. One of the assistant coaches monitored us till 9:30 or 10 at night. They were long days."

Harold eventually regained his confidence and succeeded on the hardwoods.

HAROLD JENSEN: "I met Dave Sudjian, a good friend of John Pinone's at Smokey Joe's one night. We grew to be good friends. We'd just hang out together and talk things through. Dave helped make me believe in myself. After graduation, we wound up becoming business partners when we formed Showtime Productions."

Harold also succeeded in the classroom. He was honored in 1987 by being selected to the GTE/COSIDA All-American team, awarded each year by the GTE Corporation, and voted on by the College Sports Information Directors of America. Harold joined Tom Inglesby ('73), John Pinone ('83), and Mark Plansky ('86) as the only Villanova basketballers ever to be so honored.

Harold has become a Pennsylvanian since his 'Nova experience. The big city offers some advantages in business, as it did in college.

HAROLD JENSEN: "One of the advantages of playing near a big city like Philly was that the '76ers used to stop in at the gym. We'd play pick-up games with them—guys like Dr. J, Mo Cheeks, and Charles Barkley. That was great experience. I'm amazed, I saw Charles in Las Vegas a year or so ago and he still remembers me. He was sitting at a table with Tiger Woods and some others. When I walked by, he stood up and hugged me, saying, 'I remember you from Villanova.'"

Number One

Villanova wasn't ranked in the top 20 for most of the season. Georgetown, Michigan, St. John's, Oklahoma, and Memphis State comprised the top five. The number one slot is hard to come by. In the Hoyas' history, Georgetown has been in the top spot for only eleven weeks—all in the '84-'85 season. They held the top position most of the '84-'85 campaign. When St. John's defeated them, they slipped to number two, but only for a few weeks. When they convincingly trouncing the Red Force a few weeks later, the Hoyas reascended to number one.

Villanova has never reached number-one. In March 2004, Philadelphia's St. Joseph's University was ranked number one for the first time in its rich history. Only three other Big Five teams, St. Joe's, LaSalle, and Temple, can claim a number-one ranking. The 27-0 St. Joe's Hawks ascended to the top spot at the end of the regular 2003-2004 season. LaSalle has been there twice—first in December 1952 and again in December 1954.

Temple, holds the distinction for the longest consecutive time at number one among its Big Five peers. John Chaney's Owls perched atop the AP poll for six straight weeks from February 9, 1988, up to and including the final rankings on March 15.

The Rose Garden

A few days after their April Fool surprise, the team bussed down to Washington, D.C. to meet with president Ronald Reagan. Reagan joked with the team: "You're being called a Cinderella team, but I don't see anybody here who looks like he can fit into a glass slipper." Coach Mass quipped: "We know you're a Hoya fan, but we'd like to make you an honorary Wildcat." The president shot back, "Coach, you should know I can't be a fan of anyone. You're all my constituents."

The president paid homage to the Villanova heritage. He was well prepped in Villanova lore. As he walked down the line shaking everyone's hand, President Reagan halted in front of trainer Jake Nevin and said, "I know that Monday night's victory was a bittersweet one. A person whose life was so much a part of Villanova basketball passed away that morning, Alex Severance left a long legacy, with 60 years at the university. And there's someone else here who deserves recognition—Jake

Nevin. Jake, everyone knows what you mean to this team and to all of the students at Villanova. This championship is a tribute to you and to Alex Severance. You've made your mark and your personal courage has inspired greatness."

The president summed up the thoughts of America when he said: "The eyes of the nation were on you, and you didn't buckle under the pressure. Your hands stayed steady. One of the longest moments in sports must be during a jump shot, in that fraction of a second where you're suspended in the air and crowd is yelling. You're looking for a small white cylinder that seems to be a mile away. And you have to throw the ball into that tiny net before Pat Ewing comes out of nowhere to block it."

Despite those difficulties, Mr. President, we are the champions.

Chapter Seven

POSTSCRIPT TO '85

The members of the championship squad faded slowly away from the NCAA scene. After Eddie, Dwayne, and Gary graduated in 1985, the Wildcats continued to growl. The starters included three key members of the championship squad: Pressley, Jensen, and Wilbur. Mark Plansky moved into the starting quintet and freshmen Doug West and Kenny Wilson glided seamlessly into the program. The team's record dipped to 23-14 that next season. But the script looked surprisingly—maybe promisingly—familiar. The 'Cats posted similar results versus their super-nemeses Georgetown and St. John's. They split the season series with the Hoyas. The win was a 90-88 double-overtime heart-thumper at the Palestra. Prez scintillated with 34 on 14-for-17 shooting. The "other Harold"—Jensen—added 16, and frosh flash Doug West contributed 15. As for the Red Force of New York—well, same old story. St. John's scored another trifecta over the Wildcats. The Red Force overtook them twice in the regular season, before painting them out of the Big East Tournament in the semifinals.

Rollie kept on keeping on, spinning his first-round NCAA Tournament magic yet again as the 'Cats schooled Virginia Tech in Baton Rouge. Another Techie, Georgia Tech, squelched dreams of a repeat when they caged the 'Cats in a 66-61 setback the next round.

After '86, Chuck Everson and RC Massimino bid adieu to their college days as did Harold Pressley. Prez emerged as a superstar that season. His departure cracked the 'Cat attack. In '86-'87, Jensen and Plansky were starters, but the season turned out to be a downer. The 15-16 Wildcats suffered through their

Steve Pinone played for Villanova and then joined Rollie Massimino's coaching staff after graduation. (Photo courtesy of the Villanova Sports Information Department)

Rollie Massimino coached the Wildcats to their only national championship. (Photo courtesy of the Villanova Sports Information Department)

first losing campaign in a dozen years. For the first time in seven years, the 'Cats didn't get an invitation to the Big Dance. They were invited to the NIT but were eliminated in the first round by city rival LaSalle. The 'Cats also went down to defeat in the first round of the Big East Tournament.

By the '88 season, Mark Plansky was the only 'Cat still sporting a championship ring. Mark rounded out a starting quintet of Doug West, Kenny Wilson, Rodney Taylor, and Tom Greis. 'Nova made one of its greatest postseason runs ever that year. In the Big East Tournament, Villanova was seeded number four, and finally upended St. John's, registering a first-round 71-68 triumph. Next, 'Nova squeaked past Pitt, 72-69, before losing the final to Syracuse.

Mark Plansky and Doug West both made the All-Big East squads—the first time two 'Cats had been so honored in the same year since 1981 when John Pinone and Alex Bradley did it (1997 is the only subsequent year that two 'Cats made the All-Big East team when Alvin Williams and Tim Thomas were selected).

The 'Cats made a great run in the NCAAs, too. They downed Arkansas and Illinois in the first two rounds in Cincinnati, gunning their way into the Sweet Sixteen. Then they headed to Birmingham Alabama for the Southeast Regionals. They upended Kentucky for the first and only time in Wildcat history (the all-time series is 1-5, Kentucky) to advance to the Elite Eight. Oklahoma ousted the 'Cats in the Southeast Regional final, 78-57 to dash the trip to the Final Four.

Ed and Dwayne to the NBA

After graduation in '85, Ed Pinckney and Dwayne McClain moved up to the NBA. Ed went to the Phoenix Suns, Dwayne to the Indiana Pacers. E-Z Ed eased into the NBA, playing sporadically at the start. He got his first NBA start on January 30, 1986 against the Portland Trailblazers. He responded with 24 points.

Dwayne eased into the NBA too. At the time, his Indiana team was the youngest in the league. D-Train's first big NBA night came against the Atlanta Hawks, when he exploded with 15 points.

John McLeod coached the Suns, George Irvine the Pacers.

DWAYNE McCLAIN: "Eddie and I kept in touch a lot that first season, talking about our adjustment to this level. I'm not saying our NBA coaches weren't good. They were. But we didn't appreciate till we got to the pros what a great coach Coach Mass was. He taught us what we needed to know. We already knew what some guys at the professional level don't know till they get there. Coach Mass was leading us in the right direction all along.

"I'd have to say that the biggest difference between college and pro was the atmosphere. In the NBA, the players are grown men with families apart from the game. At Villanova, the players were my family. I missed the family atmosphere we had at 'Nova."

The two Villanova stars performed on the professional hardwoods a number of years, though their paths were decidedly different. Ed traveled the NBA circuit for more than a decade, while Dwayne traveled the world, playing in Europe and Australia.

E-Z Ed, Assistant Coach

Ed Pinckney no longer shoots baskets and grabs rebounds for a living. He was a tough man to shadow on the hardwoods. He still is.

I really enjoy the life of a coach. I've had to make several adjustments. I have no free time. The whole thing just draws me in. During the season, my schedule is intense because of preparing for games, team meetings, meetings with the coaches, studying films, taking care of problems the kids have—all those things. That's to be expected. But it really never ends. Once the season's over, I'm just as busy. We prepare for the postseason banquets, step up recruiting, and take care of a million things that crop up every day. But I have to admit I love it. It's a learning experience, but I think I'm making progress.

Ed remains modest and humble. Nothing eye-catchy embellishes his office. Even the location of the office, buried deep in the subterranean labyrinth of the Jake Nevin Field House among gyms, rooms, pools, lockers, and corridors, is nondescript.

CHUCK EVERSON: "When I walked into Ed's new office at Villanova, I saw just what I expected. There were no pictures of the '85 team at all! Nothing! Ed just doesn't keep those kinds of things. He'd consider it like bragging if he hung them up on his office wall. I asked him why he didn't have any pictures of the championship team on the wall. He told me he didn't have any, which I'm sure is true. I said, 'If I make you some good copies of mine, would you hang them up?' He said he would, so I did and sent them down. He never hung them.

"I didn't expect him to. E-Z Ed was always so laid back. Nothing ever fazed him. If he asked to borrow $20, you'd give it to him happily—knowing you'd never see it again. Not that Ed didn't have every intention of repaying you, he just forgot about things like that. But if you borrowed $40 from him, he'd forget about that just as easily."

Chuck didn't mention how many times he invested $20 to earn $40, but it is a good hedge against a shaky stock market.

No one talks about E-Z Ed without some mention of the easygoing style he's always had.

TOM FLANAGAN, 1985 manager: "Ed was a guy who liked to have fun. He was completely down to earth and liked to joke around—he was just fun to hang out with. Right after he graduated, Ed stayed in my apartment for awhile, wrapping up his business here before reporting to the NBA. I was down the shore for the summer, so he had the place to himself. When I got back to the apartment after summer, Ed had gone. But he left all kinds of trophies and other memorabilia behind. I gave it all to Rollie. But I don't know that Ed ever got it again or ever missed it."

'Nova legend Wali Jones worked with Ed at the Miami Heat from 1997 through 2003.

WALI JONES: "Ed was one of the most poised kids I ever saw. His poise helped him on the basketball court. You hear about 'basketball IQ'—well, Ed had a high one. He's had poise since the moment I met him as a high school kid. His poise allowed him to make the most of his talent. He never got rattled. He's going to be a good coach because of that quality. And he has such a nice manner with the young men. He's a good mentor, a guy kids trust. They loved Ed in Miami. The whole organization did. Ed headed the mentoring program for the club his last year with us. He did a great job because of the way he comes across to the youngsters. He'll develop into a good coach at Villanova. He'll really carry on the tradition."

Chapter Eight

FAMILY MATTERS

The Villanova Family

Winning the 1985 men's basketball championship didn't land "Villa-nowhere" a spot on the national collegiate sport scene. Villanova already had one. A school that has produced forty Olympians, placed at least one student in every summer Olympics since 1948, won 16 NCAA titles, won 63 Big East Conference championships, and sent 52 baseball players to the major leagues, is hardly a Johnny-come-lately in college sports.

As Jim Murray noted, the school tends to accomplish big-time things while operating from a small-time platform. The strength of that platform does not lie in infrastructure—not in big budgets and glitzy facilities and enticing perks. The strength lies in the family. Sign in to Villanova and you commit to a family.

HARRY BOOTH: "I devoted my whole life to St. Joe's. They're a wonderful institution, and I appreciate the years I spent there. When I came to Villanova, I was apprehensive about how I'd be accepted. You know, the Hawks and Wildcats are archrivals. But I found Villanova to be a wonderful atmosphere. Jim Murray, Villanova's former sports information director, came up with a great line years ago. It went something like this, 'Take some good kids, throw in some Italian seasoning (that would be Rollie), mix in some Augustinian teaching, and stir gently for four years—that's a recipe that usually turns out a pretty good kid.' That's really the way it feels there. Athletes are treated as members of the Villanova family here, not as somebody who's above everyone else. It's a true family feeling."

You don't have to look around campus very far to start finding the family connections.

MARY ANNE GABUZDA: "I started working in the basketball office in May 1980. In fact, one of my first jobs was to type and send Ed Pinckney his recruiting letters when he was in high school. I grew up in Delaware County (adjacent to Philadelphia). I loved Villanova and I loved Villanova basketball. The place always felt like family to me, but there was good reason for that. My mother worked for Villanova all her life—till she retired in 1986. Her brother—my uncle—is the team chaplain, Father Lazor. Throw in the fact that I love sports, and then you know why I've been so happy here for so long."

ROB WILSON ("STATS"): "Mary Anne was super for us managers. I don't know how many times she drove the managers up to New England and New York when we had games there and no transportation. She was a diehard fan and a loyal supporter, and to me personally, she was a lifesaver. I couldn't type. When I had papers due for class, Mary Anne would come in early and type them for me—for free, of course. Like any college student, I couldn't pay her. I had no money. But she didn't care. She really felt like we were all family."

MARY ANNE GABUZDA: "It is like a big family here. We've had so many great kids come through the program, so many kids with caring families. Really, our program looks for those types of kids—kids who have been brought up with good values, not just kids who happen to be talented basketball players.

"The kids on the championship team are a good example. They were wonderful. We all felt as close to their parents as we did to them. I remember them all so well. Dwayne's mother was such a lovely person—and beautiful! Everyone thought she was Dwayne's sister. And the Pinone family was so warm. I got to know all the Pinones very well over the years since John and Steve both played here. Mark Plansky's parents were huge Villanova supporters. They tried to get down here for every game, every event. Even when Mark wasn't starting as a fresh-man, it didn't matter. They were here because they felt a part of Villanova. Harold Pressley's family is so nice. Prez' parents, Margaret and Russell Means, treated the team to a homecooked dinner every time we played near Mystic, Connecticut. That's their home. To this day, I stop and visit them whenever I'm in New England. Harold's sister Vanessa also attended Villanova.

"You get the idea. I could go on and on about every single one of them."

Say One for Rollie

One of Villanova's fiercest rooters attended games with Mary Anne Gabuzda.

MARY ANNE GABUZDA: "I used to drive Rollie's kids to the away games. Sister Mary Margaret Cribben always went with us. Talk about the Villanova family! She was a fixture at Villanova for years. She taught a library science course that a lot of the athletes took. They all loved her. She was crazy about every sport, not just basketball. You'd see her at football, baseball, track—everything. I'll never forget, one time we drove up to a game in New York and, since the game was going to end late in the evening, Rollie got us a room to stay over. You should have seen us getting ready before the game. Rollie's girls and I were all doing our hair and Sister was in her room praying for a win!"

Jake
Times Change. Taste Remains.

Times have changed. People come and go so quickly in jobs these days that it's doubtful that another Jake Nevin will ever pop up on the scene. Five years marks a lifetime with most employers in our enlightened age. But five and a half decades (and some change) with the same employer? I can't imagine a repeat of that story. Another Villanova team will win a national champion and shoot 100-percent without grabbing a single rebound before another Jake Nevin comes along.

But taste remains. And taste for a human being like Jake remains the same no matter what era humanity finds itself in. Nothing and no one epitomizes Villanova's "family" and family values more than Jake Nevin. It's ironic that the quintessential member of the Villanova family was himself never married, and never fathered any children. Jake's kids were Villanova students—the constant stream of hopefuls that flowed through the University year after year.

Jake's celebrity spilled out beyond Lancaster Avenue and the Main Line. The irascible old trainer won the hearts of Philadelphians. In a city that booed Santa Claus, Jake Nevin was beloved. He was inducted into the Big Five Hall of Fame, had his honorary number 1 retired, and had a Field House named after him.

HARRY BOOTH: "Jake had no formal college education, but he had a doctorate in people skills. Everyone who had anything to do with Villanova for the past 50 years has a

Jake story. That's what I heard before I arrived and that's what I found to be true. I got my own Jake story on my first trip to Villanova.

"I was nervous and worried about making the right impression so I wore a tie. That was a little too formal for Jake's taste, so he got a pair of scissors, sneaked up on me, and snipped it in half."

MARK PLANSKY: "Jake made quite an impression on me too the first time I was at Villanova. I was a high school senior. I went into the gym and ran into Jake. I didn't know who he was, but I was trying to be polite to everyone. Jake started asked me, 'Who are you?' Every time I anwered 'Mark Plansky,' he'd ask again, 'Who?' I was only a high school kid taking everything seriously, and I'm wondering what's wrong with this guy. He finally let me off the hook, and I realized he was kidding.

"The point is: Jake didn't wait long to pull a joke on you, even if it was only the old cigar-butt-in-the-sneaker trick. Sooner or later, Jake busted every Villanova athlete on that one."

Trick or Treat?

MARK PLANSKY: "When I met Jake, it was close to Halloween. I was standing in the gym, watching practice, just making conversation with him when Jake asks, 'Know what I'm going out as on Halloween?' I said, 'No, Jake. What?' Jake winked, 'I'm going out as a fireman. Yeah, I'm just gonna throw my hose over my shoulder and go.'

Jake couldn't resist a good quip even if the straight man happened to be the president of the United States.

MARK PLANSKY: When we were in the Rose Garden, President Reagan said, 'Jake, it's a pleasure to meet you.' Jake didn't miss a beat when he shot back, 'Mr. President, the pleasure is all yours!'"

Mr. Reagan, meet the Villanova family.

Rollie

Family matters. That doesn't sum Rollie Massimino up. But it does provide a prism to view a multifaceted personality. All his players and staff wax eloquent that basketball was life in the Rollie philosophy—meaning that Coach Mass was adept at using basketball to teach universal lessons. Oh sure, Rollie was a tactician, astute in the sport he chose as his lifetime profession. But what he strived to do most of all was to instill values like responsibility, commitment, and loyalty—team behaviors for all of life's endeavors. And in the Coach Mass philosophy, those virtues take root best in the special soil of family love.

Whitey Rigsby played on Massimino's early Villanova teams. He's been announcing Wildcat games for a number of years.

WHITEY RIGSBY: "I felt so happy for Rollie when we won the '85 championship. See—I say we, not he or they. That's the way Rollie wants it. I'll never forget what he told me at four a.m. in his room at the Ramada the morning after we beat Georgetown. Rollie pulled Joe Rogers and me aside. Joe and I roomed together in college. Joe played for Archbishop Carroll in Philly. He was the first guy Rollie recruited after Rollie got to Villanova. Rollie told us, 'I really want to thank you guys. You deserve as much credit as anyone for this championship. Guys like you built our program. You made it a success, something that would carry on—something that could lead to this championship.'

"I was really moved. At this incredibly triumphant moment for the man when he's in the spotlight, he's thanking two guys who haven't played for him for over a decade. He's crediting us for helping to make this championship happen. We considered ourselves nothing more than alumni, just spectators like everyone else. But Rollie has such a fundamental belief in family. He viewed Joe and me as an earlier generation of the family. And to Rollie, without our generation, the Ed Pinckney generation would not have been possible, nor would it have succeeded."

Merry Christmas

VIC D'ASCENZO: "Rollie's sense of family keeps him busy every Christmas. Do you know he calls all his former players at Christmas to wish them the best of the season? I know. I helped him get everybody's phone number."

The Real Rollie

The public saw a different Rollie than did his players, his family. To the public, Rollie was all gesticulations, animation, and fire.

WHITEY RIGSBY: "It wasn't easy for Rollie to follow Jack Kraft. Jack appealed to the Main Liners. He was a subdued, low key guy. Main Line is Brooks Brothers and button-downs, and Jack fit right in. Now, along comes Rollie with his crumpled suits, arms waving all over the place and yelling. We had some bad teams when Rollie first arrived, and people weren't used to Villanova losing. They weren't too happy about it, either. But Rollie was committed. He stuck with his program and it paid dividends in the end."

Rollie's program was exhausting. He was always on the road scouting a prospect or meeting with his family. Rollie the recruiter was a whirlwind. Ed Pinckney's mom felt the power. It took only one Rollie visit with the Pinckneys for Mrs. Pinckney to be sold on Villanova: "That little Italian coach," she told her son, "He'll make sure you graduate."

WHITEY RIGSBY: "I'll never forget when Rollie recruited me. My parents and I were inexperienced, kind of wide-eyed about the whole thing. We had no idea what to expect. Then here comes this dervish in a $750 suit rolling into our living room. Rollie always looked terrific and dressed well when he represented the school. Anyway, he charges in and plops right down on our Ottoman. He's calling me 'Robert' and waving his arms as he talks, and he ends up toppling off the Ottoman right down on his butt. But he never breaks stride, never stops talking! He just hoists himself back up on the Ottoman and keeps going. I was scared of him already!"

It was a healthy "scared." Most of Rollie's players felt that little twinge of awe peppered with a pinch of fear. But the "scared" feeling was born of respect and a desire to please—the same way a kid wants to please his dad. Many of Rollie's players characterize him as a strict, sometimes stubborn man who, at heart, had a big heart. Rollie was the father figure, "Daddy Mass."

WHITEY RIGSBY: "Kids might be intimidated at first by Rollie. But that was healthy. I believe that every kid trusted Rollie and felt they could talk to him honestly. One on one, Rollie was as good as anyone I've ever seen.

"Rollie took a personal interest in each kid. He wanted them all to succeed. I always felt he was looking out for me. I'll give you an example. I was benched for a while when I got to Villanova. I had always played on good teams in high school and I always started. Now here I was in college—I'm on a bad team and I'm not starting. I was having a tough time dealing with it, so I went to his office. He sat me down and we talked. No screaming, no intimidation. He listened. Then he listed ten things I needed to do to improve. I walked out thinking, 'This guy has thought this out! He's given me personal attention. He knows what he's talking about. He's right. I do need to improve in every area he mentioned.' Talking with him lifted me up, made me feel good—even though the message was not all rosy. He gave me a focus and made me improve."

Rollie demanded that his coaching staff nurture the same kind of paternal, one-on-one relationship with the kids.

"Rollie and his coaches devoted whatever time was necessary for a kid to develop. That's why it was great to be a basketball player at Villanova. They worked with me on developing a power game, taught me to play post, and worked on my perimeter game.

"The coaches split up and each one worked with a different group. Believe it or not, Rollie was the one that worked with the big guys. Yeah, funny huh? I don't know how a little guy like Rollie learned all those big-man moves. But he knew them. And, whenever anybody had questions, Rollie wasn't one of those guys who tell you, 'See me after practice and I'll explain it to you.' No, Rollie worked it all out then and there, move by move. He made his coaches do the same. You could always expect any of our coaches to give you his undivided attention on any problem on or off the court.

Breeazoids

Rollie was a daunting figure for 18-year-olds on their own for the first time.

HAROLD JENSEN: "I was really worried about my first practice. Fall practice started on October 15. My freshman year, Steve Pinone, John Branca (a team manager nicknamed "Wolfman" for reasons too dicey to get into), and I got our hands on World Series tickets for the Phillies game the night before Villanova practice was to start. The three of us traveled down to the Vet and got back to campus real late. I was worried that I was going to be tired and make a bad impression at my first college practice. It turns out practice went OK, but it took a few days to catch up on my sleep."

One thing Rollie hated more than being tired at practice was having spectators, particularly female spectators.

HAROLD JENSEN: "Rollie's practices were intense. He kicked everyone out of the stands. And he particularly didn't like women hanging around. He called them 'Breeazoids.' Don't ask. I don't know where the word comes from, but I heard it a lot."

Family Involvement

Rollie and his staff were there for their kids, their family. They sacrificed to maintain that level of commitment.

HARRY BOOTH: "I was a volunteer coach. I couldn't make practice every day because I worked another job full time. Rollie kept me totally involved, though. He insisted that I come to his house whenever I couldn't make practice. I did. I'd stop on my way home. Rollie's wife would cook up some 'spags.' Then I'd go back to my own house and my wife would have another dinner prepared for me. I had to keep hustling all the time, but that was Rollie's idea of family, commitment, devotion, and all the things that he thought mattered."

MARK PLANSKY: "I'll tell you how much 'family' means to Rollie Massimino. When my father died a few years ago—long after my days at Villanova—Coach Mass flew up here to Boston for the funeral. When I saw the Coach, he offered his condolences and apologized because he couldn't stay long. I was moved by the fact that Rollie would take all that time off. I know first-hand that Rollie is one busy man! But he put paying his last respects to my father ahead of everything else, 'cause he considered my father was family.

"I grew to have tremendous respect for Rollie. My dad was the biggest influence on my life, but Coach Mass was next. He was a role model."

CHUCK EVERSON: "I'd call my dad the number-one influence on my life and Rollie the number 1A. I coach kids' teams now and find myself constantly telling them the same things Rollie said to me.

"Rollie demanded attention. He's the kind of person you listen to, and fortunately he delivered proper messages.

"I met Rollie way back. I played at his camp in the Poconos in the summer and decided then I wanted to play for him. I told my dad when I was still an underclassman in high school that I wanted to go to Villanova."

STEVE PINONE: "I owe so much to Coach Mass. I became a basketball coach because of him. He gave me my first job when I joined his staff at 'Nova. His willingness to take on hard things and go the extra mile taught me lifelong lessons. Rollie worked hard. He thought nothing of driving four and a half hours a night to scout a recruit or visit his family. He made a total commitment to his team and his school."

Rollie was demanding, and those demands were attached to consequences.

HARRY BOOTH: "That Pittsburgh game where Rollie sat the starters down says a lot about Rollie's value system. He was willing to lose that game to teach a lesson. He did things like that more than most people realize. I can't tell you how many times he would sit someone down because he missed a class or a practice. If somebody broke the rules, he suffered consequences, and those consequences impacted the team—the family. Ultimately if one guy fell down, he brought the team down too. He wanted to teach them they carried that responsibility."

MARK PLANSKY: "I was visiting campus as a high school senior, watching the team practice. All of a sudden, Rollie kicks Eddie off the court and tells me to go in and rebound for him! He wasn't pleased with the way Ed was doing something. Eddie just smiled at me, like, 'Yeah that's the way he is.' Rollie's program was clear: no one player was bigger than the team."

Spare Me the Star Treatment?

When Sparky Anderson took control of the Big Red Machine of the seventies, there's baseball legend that has Pete Rose telling him: "There's a lot of stars in this locker room. When you need to yell at one of them, don't. They'll only pout and play worse. Yell at me instead. The others will get the message. They know how hard I play, and they'll figure they should hustle more if I'm getting my ass chewed."

Ed Pinckney never suggested that ploy to Coach Mass. It was quite the contrary. But in a way, Pinckney became the guy who got—well, not picked on—but ...

Practices were awful for me. I'm kidding about that. Really I enjoyed them. But Rollie was on my case from beginning to end. He'd stop practices and tell everyone we were starting practice over—because Pinckney isn't doing things right. He was all over me all the time. The other guys would look at me and kind of shake their heads. And we'd go back to the beginning—stretching, calisthenics, and all that.

Pat Riley did the same thing. He would pick on our biggest stars, Hardaway and Mourning, more than anyone. He did the same things to them that Rollie did to me at Villanova.

Rollie's Rules

CRAIG MILLER: "Rollie was strict and uncompromising about certain things. I remember when the NCAA was trying to come up with a drug policy based on progressive discipline. Rollie's position was firm, 'There are no second chances. Do it once and you're done. What message does progressive discipline deliver? If you do drugs once, it's OK? Well, one time is not OK.'

"Rollie had his share of strong opinions. Punctuality was another. Anyone who didn't show up on time would find the team bus gone. Rollie even left the chaplain, Father Lazor, behind once when he was late!

"One time Eddie missed the bus for the Meadowlands. I saw Ed at the hotel and gave him money for a taxi. When Ed arrived at the Meadowlands and Rollie saw him in the locker room, Rollie said, 'Don't bother getting dressed. You're not playing.' Ed explained to Rollie that he was stranded in an elevator that broke down. Rollie telephoned the hotel and found out Eddie's story was true. Rollie relented and told Ed he'd let him play, but he still wasn't going to start him because, 'You didn't leave early enough to start.'"

Rollie made those tough decisions on his own, but he was not a dictator who refused to listen.

CHUCK EVERSON: "Here's how much Rollie believed in instilling a sense of family. Rollie always assigned a particular player to show a high school recruit around and introduce him to the rest of the team. Once the recruit went back home, Rollie gathered the team together on the bench and asked each guy what he thought of the kid. Was he a good fit? Did the guys feel comfortable with him, and did they think the kid would feel comfortable at Villanova? If the team's answer came back no, it didn't matter how much basketball talent he had, Rollie wouldn't give him an offer. You hear the term 'team chemistry' a lot, but Coach Mass believed in getting the chemistry right, and he involved us in the process."

MARK PLANSKY: "It's true. Coach Mass actually let us vote on recruits. And he stuck with the team's decision. Only once do I remember him overruling us. Eric Leslie came to campus for a visit. We all agreed that Eric was a good kid and a talented player, but we didn't think he'd be a good fit for

Villanova's Twin Towers, Chuck Everson and Wyatt Maker, hoist Rollie Massimino on their shoulders at Rupp Arena. (Photo courtesy of the Villanova Sports Information Department)

the team. Rollie pursued him anyway. Eric came to Villanova but wound up transferring to URI. So I guess Rollie's system worked! I don't know any other coach who would put that much faith in his players' input."

Movin' On Up

Coach Massimino believed in bringing his key players into strategy sessions as they matured into leaders.

MARK PLANSKY: "I wasn't involved with Rollie and the team strategy much as a freshman, the year we won the championship. The whole ride was a little unreal to me. One year I'm a high school senior watching the NCAA final on TV. A year later, I'm suited up for the game in front of a worldwide audience. But I was just a bit player that year.

"Coach Mass involved me in strategy more and more every year. He had a formal goal-oriented system. He wrote down the goals—how many wins we should get, where we should finish in the Big East, what seed we should get in the NCAA. Coach Mass would tell the coaching staff and the team leaders things like, 'In our next three games, we've got to come away with two wins. They're all Big East games and two wins sets us up for the tournament.' Rollie kept his team leaders and the coaching staff focused and on the same page all season long."

Rollie the Psychologist

HARRY BOOTH: "I wish I had worked under Rollie before I started coaching. I think I would have been a better coach. Rollie said that coaching was all about handling people. He was right. Rollie was a master psychologist. The way he handled the Al Severance tragedy proves that.

"Rollie gathered the team together and broke the news about Al's death. He went into a speech about what Al Severance meant to the Villanova basketball tradition and how they were now representing that tradition. He told them Al would be up in heaven guiding our shots in and keeping Georgetown's shots out.

"That night at the pregame dinner, he told the kids to go back to their rooms and focus on what they were going to do to help their team win, because, 'We are going to win this game.'

"Rollie had great insight into people, but he could also prepare for an opponent better than anyone I've met. If I had to pick one coach for one big game—especially if there were no shot clock and no three-point shot—it would be Rollie."

Al Elia was the Wildcat public address announcer from '77 to '96. He was also the photographer for Villanova's road games from the mid-'70s to the early '80s. Al admires Rollie's people skills, but cites Rollie's people needs as an equal force.

AL ELIA: "Rollie wanted or needed people around him all the time. When I was the announcer at 'Nova, we used to kid about Rollie's 'Designated Italian' guest for the evening. It was Perry Como one night, which was a thrill for me. As a kid, Perry was one of my idols! Perry made my day when he stopped by to see me and told me, 'I love your work, Al.' Well Rollie made sure I announced that 'Coach Massimino's *good friend*, Perry Como, is in the house tonight.' Mario Andretti was Rollie's guest a few times, too. The funniest recollection I have is about Tommy Lasorda. Tommy's language tends to be, let's say, colorful. Tommy was sitting on the bench close by my mike. All night long, I was on my guard, making sure Tommy's 'colorful' comments didn't blast out over the PA."

Now That's Italian

Bob Vetrone was "Buck the Bartender" for years. "Buck" was a popular sports column that first appeared on August 15, 1977 in the *Philadelphia Bulletin*. As Bob recalls with precision, the Bulletin died at 11 a.m. on January 29, 1982. But "Buck the Bartender" lived on. The *Philadelphia Daily News* picked the column up and ran it till December 23, 1992.

Bob introduced the column when "trivia was getting big" (Bob observes, "That's an oxymoron, isn't it?"). In his sportswriting days, Bob used to cover Villanova. As an Italian-American who couldn't speak Italian, Vetrone came under fire from Rollie. Bob's father owned a butcher shop in South Philly. His dad spoke Italian, but Bob never learned it. Rollie was constantly working Bob over about not speaking Italian. One day, Rollie wore trousers that had 'Sergio Valente' on the rear pocket, Bob told Rollie he was studying Italian. Rollie said, 'Really?' Bob answered, "Yeah. I know what 'Sergio Valente' means. It means 'fat ass.'"

Emotions and Outbursts

Dodger manager Lasorda made no bones about showing his reactions and emotions. Neither did Coach Mass.

WHITEY RIGSBY: "In Rollie's second year, we were playing in the Kentucky Invitational. I thought Rollie broke his foot. He kicked a metal Coke container so hard that he broke it. Rollie's reputation must have preceded him. The next night, they gave us a Styrofoam container instead."

VIC D'ASCENZO: "Rollie, the coaches, and the managers used to play pick-up games after practice. Rollie was as intense in those games as he was when he was coaching. Actually, I've got to admit Rollie could shoot the ball. He used to hit a mid-lane jumper all the time. As for fouls, that's a different story. According to Rollie, he never fouled me, but every move I made was a foul, according to him.

"No matter what he was doing, he never lost sight of the fact that he was 'Coach Mass.' He didn't want anyone else to lose sight of it either. One time—and only one time—I made the mistake of calling him 'Rollie' while we were playing a pick-up game. It never happened again. No one called him Rollie. It was always Coach or Coach Mass, and his wife was Mrs. Mass."

I Love You Guys Too Much

Besides players, coaches, team managers and other Villanova people, Rollie's "family" extended to a select group of others.

STEVE PINONE: "You've got to mention two other members of the 'family'—Bob and Marie Domenick. Bob and Marie bleed Villanova blue and white. They've been season-ticket holders since 1946. The Domenics owned Wayne Beverage, which is no longer in operation. It used to be up Lancaster Pike, west of the campus. Bob and Marie became Coach Mass's close friends. They were terrific to the guys on the team. The Domenics used to invite all the players to their house for great pasta dinners. They were always there for us, always available to talk to for help and support. I worked for them a couple of summers while I was a student. They were just, well—family to all of us."

The Nets

Build a better mousetrap and the world will beat a path to your door. Win a national championship and they'll beat your door down. The world was beating Rollie's door down after the '85 miracle. The New York Nets were wooing Rollie hot and heavy, which titillated the Philly press. Rumors were flying everywhere: Rollie was stayng, Rollie was going.

ROB WILSON ("STATS"): "At a banquet after the season, Rollie stood up and said he wasn't sure whether he'd be staying at Villanova or not. Next day, we all waited for him at his office. I think the Coach tipped Jake off before he announced his decision to everyone else. Coach Mass looked at us all and said, 'I love you guys too much. I can't leave.' It took a minute to sink in. Then everyone started running around screaming and hugging one another."

MARK PLANSKY: "I'll never forget the day Rollie told us all he was staying at Villanova. We had gone to a dinner the night before, which turned into a roast of Rollie. Everyone in the city was talking about Rollie taking a job with the Nets. He shook hands with all of us after the dinner, and didn't tip off his decision but we were sure he was leaving. He walked into his office next morning and said, 'I love you guys too much. I'm staying.'

"I don't know for sure but I think Jake influenced Coach Mass to stay. Jake was so honest and frank. He was one of the few people who could confront Coach on that issue. I believe he told Rollie, 'I never took you for a guy who would take the money and run.'

"You know what? Whether the public knows it or not, Rollie was not one of those guys. He had a sincere love of the kids and the school—and Jake. And Rollie didn't want to let any of them down."

No Playing Not to Lose

JIM DELORENZO: "I think the greatest attribute that Rollie brought to that team, the greatest thing he instilled in them, was the ability to have fun when they were in big games. Rollie had more fun down at the Final Four than any other coach I could possibly imagine. He loved every minute of it. Some of that has to do with the era. It was more innocent back then— innocent in the sense that college basketball and the Final Four weren't such a business. Rollie still motivated those guys, told them to play to win. He made a big distinction between playing to win rather than playing not to lose. Rollie didn't want the pageantry to paralyze the kids. He saw to it that it didn't. He managed to keep the whole team loose because he wanted everyone to have fun. It's a delicate balance, but Rollie achieved it in the Final Four."

Rollie Aids

It was a night that tries coaches' souls. The 2003-2004 Wildcats had committed 25 turnovers against Virginia Tech. After the game, Ed Pinckney and five other ex-Villanova basketball players were commiserating (the names are being withheld to protect them). The time was about one in the morning. Then someone came up with the idea to telephone Coach Mass—an idea that falls squarely into the it-seemed-like-a-good-idea-at-the-time category.

Coach Massimino always told me, 'Call me anytime.' So, I was feeling down about the way we played. We all were. We just wanted to talk it out with Rollie. I guess we didn't take into account that he was 20 years older at this point, and he might have gone to bed.

Rollie's wife answered the phone and politely said that Rollie was in bed. Ed didn't ask for a callback.

A Game for the Ages

Someone recently referred to the "Curse of Villanova" in a Philadelphia sport article. "It's the Curse of Billy Penn." Billy Penn might have some celestial clout and a hankering for a payback to the city he used to overlook. Or maybe he brought a Napoleon complex into the great beyond. With Jim Thome and Donovan McNabb in town, Billy's voodoo is not going to hold out much longer. But a "Villanova Curse"—hardly! One ugly night long ago, a band of ruffians drove the Augustinians out of the City of Brotherly Love to the green pastures of the Main Line. That was then. This is now. Philly today loves that '85 'Nova crew.

HARRY BOOTH: "The '85 team appealed to Philadelphia because Philadelphia likes hard-working people who put 'we' ahead of 'I.' I'll be honest with you—going into the '85 NCAA Tournament, none of the coaches thought we had a chance. But our kids pulled it off because of discipline and desire.

"Everything about that team endeared them to Philly. I played here all my life. I know what Philly people like to see, and they saw it in this gang. These guys played with intensity and intelligence. They weren't the most talented team. But that's just what makes them special to the people in this town.

"Georgetown's philosophy and game plan was to intimidate people. They were enormously successful implementing that plan. But Rollie refused to be intimidated. He passed that toughness on to his players.

"Above all, his players were good kids—respectful and courteous. They had a freshness and airiness that made the victory over the big bad Georgetown empire all the more gratifying to the fans."

MARY ANNE GABUZDA: "The press loved that team. They were all nice kids who respected adults. They were great Villanova ambassadors on campus and off. They loved meeting the alumni. They came from caring families.

"I got as close to their families as I did to the kids. The parents still keep in touch with us. Wyatt's (Wyatt Maker) father was always calling and asking for brochures and anything else that had to do with Villanova. He's still our biggest West Coast ambassador. He came to Villanova every chance he got, even after Wyatt had graduated."

Everyone in and around Philly savored the Wildcats win. People all over the nation called it a miracle, and everyone loves a miracle. But the people who treasure that win most of all are the members of Rollie's Villanova family. After all, they're the

The 1985 National Champions. (Photo courtesy of the Villanova Sports Information Department)

ones who, on April Fool's Day in 1985, played a game for the ages.

STEVE PINONE: That championship influenced everything the rest of my life. It was such a significant achievement for a group of guys who were given no chance to succeed. An experience like that bonds you for a lifetime. It's a tremendous feeling. It gives everyone a reason to keep in touch forever. And we do.

"We had a diverse bunch—blacks, whites, inner-city kids, suburban kids, kids from the East Coast and West Coast. When all is said and done, everything we worked hard for and everything we believed in came together for us one night. We accomplished something that night that fascinates people 20 years later."

Chapter Nine

BASKETBALL
ACCOMPLISHMENTS

THE PLAYERS

Special thanks to Chuck Everson for helping to track people down. Chuck tries to surprise each of his teammates annually with a happy birthday call. Those annual calls help him keep posted on everyone's whereabouts, a task as difficult as stopping a D-Train dunk. Chuck held on to the calendar Craig Miller put together 20 years ago—the one that lists everyone on the team's birthday. Years change, birth dates don't.

Connally Brown
Nickname: B-B

Connally was born on March 26, 1965, in Orange, Texas. He starred at West Orange High School, where he made All-Region, All-District, All-Tournament, and second-team All-State in his junior and senior years. Connally was also a member of the Texas State championship track team.

Connally played in 21 games that '84-'85 championship season. He scored ten points, and grabbed ten rebounds against Pitt. He averaged 1.3 points per game and shot 52.9 percent from the field.

Veltra Dawson
Nickname: 3 D

Veltra was raised in Highland Park, Illinois. In high school, he earned All-County, All-Area, and All-Conference honors three times. In his senior year, he was All-State and honorable mention All-American averaging 24.7 points, 8.2 rebounds, 6.5 assists and three steals per game. He graduated as one of the Top 50 Outstanding Students at Highland Park High.

Veltra, an accounting major, played in 18 of 35 games as a freshman in '84-'85. He scored five against Penn and five against Brigham Young. He dished off four assists in his collegiate debut when the Wildcats won their one-thousandth game against Vermont.

Chuck Everson
Nickname: 3 D

Chuck, whose brother Steve played roundball at Lafayette College, was born in Brooklyn. Chuck attended Ross High School in Brentwood, New York, where he was the team MVP, All-Long Island, All-League, and All-Suffolk County. He was also a Street & Smith honorable-mention All-American and honorable-mention All-Stater. In his senior year, he averaged 18.7 rebounds, 22.7 points, seven blocked shots and five assists per game.

As a freshman at Villanova, Chuck appeared in 17 games in the '82-'83 season. His top game was against Temple where he netted six, pulled down five rebounds, and handed off two assists. In '83-'84, as a sophomore, Chuck, a Marketing major, scored a team-high 13 against Georgetown to go along with six rebounds in only 19 minutes of action. He also recorded nine points and nine rebounds against Loyola.

In the '84-'85 championship season, Chuck's season scoring high was eight against Marist. In other appearances, Chuck cleared six rebounds against Brigham Young and six more against Pitt. He was a member of the 1985 Big East Conference team that toured Yugoslavia and was the team's second leading scorer averaging 13.8 points per game. The summer after the national championship, Chuck was the second leading scorer on the 1985 Big East Conference Team that toured Yugoslavia, averaging 13.8 points per game.

Brian Harrington

Brian was born in Yonkers, New York. He attended Iona Prep in New Rochelle, New York. Brian majored in English at Villanova. He was a freshman walk-on in 1981-'82, and one of two walk-ons on the NCAA championship team.

Harold Jensen
Nicknames: Norman, Norm, Headeronomous, Howie

Harold was born in Bridgeport, Connecticut. He was a consensus high school All-American at Trumbull High School his senior year. Harold was an All-State and All-Conference selection for two years, the MVP of the Conference Playoffs for two years, and the Bridgeport Post MVP of the All-Region team for two years. Harold captained the U.S. team that played in the Albert Schweitzer International Basketball Tournament in Germany. He was awarded the Daughters of the American Revolution Citizenship Leadership Award in his senior year in high school when he averaged 23 points, 8.2 rebounds, five assists, and 4.7 steals per game.

At Villanova, Harold played in 30 of 31 games his freshman year ('83-'84), starting in three of them. His best effort as a rookie was 18 points, which earned him a Big East Rookie of the Week honor.

Harold was a sophomore that championship season. He hit for double figures six times that year, His highlights include the game-winning lay-up against Dayton; 10 second-half points on five of six shooting against North Carolina (which earned him the CBS/ Chevrolet Villanova MVP award), and 14 points (a

Harold Jensen, today, is the successful Chief Relationship Officer and Executive Vice President of Showtime Enterprises. (Photo courtesy of the Villanova Sports Information Department)

season high) against Georgetown in the NCAA championship tilt. He missed three games in '84-'85 with a broken bone in his left hand, but returned for an awesome post-season.

Here's What D-Train Sends Along to Harold

DWAYNE McCLAIN, "I nicknamed Harold 'Norm' when we played, cause Harold had that look about him, kind of intense and scary like Norman Bates. I got together with Harold this past year when I came back to Philly. He's still Norman Bates!"

Wyatt Maker
Nickname: Nan

Wyatt was born to an athletic family in San Francisco. His brother Bill started at outside linebacker for Rhode Island's football team, and his brother Mike played guard on Hartnel Junior College's basketball squad. Wyatt left a fabulous legacy at North Salinas High in Salinas, California. He was selected to the All-Central Coast and All-Northern California teams. He was the 1982 Central Coast Section scoring and rebounding leader and was chosen to the All-Monterey Bay League team for three years. In his senior year, he was MVP of the Monterey Bay League when he averaged 25.5 points, 17.1 rebounds, and five assists per game. He graduated from North Salinas High as its all-time leading scorer and rebounder.

As a Villanova freshman, Wyatt appeared in 19 games, scoring a season-high six against Seton Hall. He scored in five other games, while shooting at a 54-percent clip. He sat out the entire '83-'84 season with a stress fracture in his right foot.

In the '84-'85 championship campaign, he saw action in 19 games, scoring a season-high 11 against Temple.

R.C. Massimino

R.C. attended Marple-Newtown High School in Pennsylvania where he was selected to the All-Central League team and the All-Delaware County second team. R.C. was the third leading scorer in the Central League his senior year. He was also an excellent student—a four-year member of the Honor Roll and a member of the National Honor Society.

As a Villanova freshman, R.C. saw action in 14 games in the '82-'83 season. As a sophomore, he appeared 15 times. In the '84-'85 championship campaign, R.C., a civil engineering major, appeared in 17 games, scoring three points each against Pitt, Seton Hall, and Vermont.

Dwayne McClain
Nickname: D-Train

D-Train, one of ten children of Walter and Lorener McClain, was born in Worcester, Massachusetts. Dwayne attended Holy Name High School in Worcester and made honorable mention on both the Adidas and McDonald's All-American teams. He was picked as one of All-Star Sports Top 90 Recruits, and twice made the All-Massachusetts team. Dwayne was named to the All-Central New England squad and the Boston Shootout All-Star team. He was honored as Holy Name's Athlete of the Year in his junior year. In his senior year, he received the Athletic Achievement Award.

At Villanova, Dwayne, a marketing major, was a freshman *Basketball Weekly* honorable-mention All-American. He was selected to the Big East Conference All-Rookie team. As a sophomore, he played for the Big East team that toured Italy, Spain, and Yugoslavia during the summer. His 13 points per game (on 63 percent shooting) was the squad's second highest. As a junior, he made the All-Big East third team and the All-UAB Classic tournament team. He won the CBS/Chevrolet Villanova MVP of the Villanova-Arkansas game.

D-Train was the Wildcats' '84-'85 tri-captain along with Ed Pinckney and Gary McLain.

Here's What Mark Plansky Sends
Along to Dwayne

MARK PLANSKY: "When we rode the bus back from the Rupp Auditorium after beating Georgetown, we were all singing, 'We Are the Champions.' Wayne was leading the song, doing his best Freddy Mercury impression."

When reminded that Dwayne has started a record company in Australia, Mark had this to say: "Dwayne'll do well. He always succeeds unless ... look, he's not thinking of getting behind the mic, himself, is he? If he is, forget that "always succeeds stuff.""

Gary McLain
Nickname: Gizmo, Giz

Gary, son of Lorenzo and Geneva Garett, was born in Tarrytown, New York. He attended Methuen High School in Massachusetts. Giz was honorable-mention Adidas All-American, as well as All-State for two years, All-Merrimac Valley Conference for three years, and a Boston Shootout All-Star. In his senior year at Methuen High, he averaged 14 points and eight assists per game.

As a Villanova freshman, Gary, a Communications Arts major, handed out 13 assists, the ninth highest in Wildcat annals, against St. John's in the ECAC Holiday Festival Finals. After freshman year, he played for the Big East All-Star team that toured Angola, averaging 11 points per game for the tour. As a sophomore, he won the NBC/Chevrolet Villanova MVP award against Syracuse for his 16 points and three steals.

Against North Carolina, he poured in 10 points and had no turnovers in the Cats big win. As a junior, he twice won the NBC/Chevrolet Villanova MVP—once against Syracuse and once against Notre Dame.

Gary was a tri-captain of the '84-'85 NCAA champs.

Ed Pinckney
Nickname: E-Z Ed

Ed was born in the Bronx, son of Edward and Celesta Pinckney. The couple had seven daughters. Ed was the only son. He attended Adlai E. Stevenson High School where he was a consensus All-America a senior. He was All-State and All-City his junior and senior years. Ed graduated from Adlai Stevenson as their all-time leading scorer and rebounder. In his senior year, he averaged 20.9 points, 17 rebounds, 4.6 blocked shots, and 3.5 assists per game, while shooting an amazing 75 percent from the floor.

As a Villanova freshman, Ed was a consensus freshman All-American, as well as an NCAA Eastern Regional All-Tournament selection, an All-Big East Tournament selection, and an All-Big East Rookie Team selection. He was the fifth most accurate overall field goal shooter at 64 percent. Ed also made the 1982 National Sports Festival East Team, copping the MVP and averaging 19.3 points, 17 rebounds, 4.6 blocked shots, and 3.5 assists per game to complement his glitzy 65 percent marksmanship from the field.

As a sophomore, E-Z Ed was a second-team All-American choice of *Basketball Times*. He made the All-Big East first team, the All-Philadelphia Big Five first team, and the All-UAB Tournament Team. He was the NBC/Chevrolet Villanova MVP twice—once in the ill-fated Houston game and the other against Lamar.

As a junior, Ed was one of ten finalists for the John R. Wooden Award, an honorable mention All-American, an All-Big East second-team selection, an All-Philadelphia Big Five team member, an All-East pick, and an All-UAB Tournament selection. Ed starred on the Big East team that toured Yugoslavia, averaging 14 points per game.

As a senior, Ed, a communications arts major, led the 'Cats to their first and only national championship.

Steve Pinone

Steve is the youngest of John and Alice Pinone's three children. Steve's older brother John is a former Villanova All-American. Steve attended South Catholic High School in Hartford Connecticut where he made the All-Hartford County second team. He was South Catholic's team captain his senior year. South Catholic lost the state semifinals three straight years by one point in overtime. Steve also made All-Conference in baseball as a pitcher and first baseman.

Steve, a finance major, was a basketball team walk-on at Villanova. He played nine games as a freshman and nine games as a sophomore for the NCAA champs.

Mark Plansky

Mark, the son of Bernard and Madeleine Plansky, is one of seven children. He attended Wakefield High School in Massachusetts, where he earned honorable-mention All-American laurels and All-State honors for three years. Twice he was selected the Massachusetts Division II Player of the Year, Three times he was picked as Middlesex League MVP. Mark graduated as the all-time leading scorer and rebounder at his high school. He was also a top student, graduating second in a class of 380. A member of the National Honor Society, he achieved a 3.75 grade-point average.

In his freshman season in '84-'85, Mark, an electrical engineering major at 'Nova, appeared in 30 games. He missed four games due to arthroscopic knee surgery. His best game came against Seton Hall, where he netted 12 and grabbed four rebounds. He also hit for nine against St. John's, while packaging eight points with six rebounds against Temple.

Harold Pressley
Nicknames: Prez or Coz

Harold is one of five children of Russell and Margaret Means. He was born in the Bronx, and attended St. Bernard High School in Uncasville, Connecticut. Harold was a consensus Prep School All-American and three-time All-Stater. He made All-League four times and was selected MVP at both the Five-Star and B/C basketball camps. Harold led his high school to state titles in both his junior and senior years. He finished his high school career as his school's all-time leading scorer and rebounder.

At Villanova, Prez started 22 times as a freshman, racking up a season-high 10 points, 10 rebounds, and five assists against Marist. As a sophomore, he blossomed into an honorable mention All-American. He won the CBS/Chevrolet Villanova team MVP Award in the Wildcat-St. John's game. He also scored 26 to go along with 10 boards in capturing the Coca-Cola Meadowlands MVP in the Seton Hall contest.

As a junior on the '84-'85 champs, Harold, an administrative science major, was selected to the NCAA Southeast Regional All-Tournament team and Cotton States Kiwanis Classic All-Tournament team. He posted 22 points with eight rebounds against Boston College, and 19 points and 13 boards against Penn. Harold topped 'Nova 14 times in rebounding that season. He averaged 12 points (third best on team) and 7.1 rebounds (second best on team) per game. He was second in blocked shots and third in assists. Harold topped the 'Cats in minutes played (1,191).

Dwight Wilbur
Nickname: Dee

Dwight, the son of Paul and Liz Wilbur, was born in Paterson, New Jersey. He attended Don Bosco Tech where he made All-State and honorable-mention All-America. He was a two-time All-State Parochial pick, a three-time All-Passaic County pick, and a three-time All-League honoree. He graduated as Don Bosco's all-time leading scorer.

As a Villanova freshman, Dwight, a communications arts major, played in 23 of 32 games, with two starts. As a sophomore on the '82-'83 team, he played in all 31 games. His buzzer-beater against Georgetown that year opened the door to the

'Cats' overtime victory. As a member of the Big East All-Star team that toured Yugoslavia that summer, Dwight averaged 8.5 ppg.

In 'Nova's championship season, Dwight started 34 of 35 games at guard, and reached double figures 12 times. He tallied 20 against Brigham Young, 19 against Pitt, and 18 against Providence. Dwight was fifth on the team in scoring and fourth in rebounding.

THE COACHES

Rollie Massimino
See the Appendix for Rollie's accomplishments.

Mitch Buonaguro

Mitch was an All-City player at Bishop Loughlin High School in Brooklyn. He played college ball at Boston College from '71-'75, graduating cum laude in history. After graduation, he stayed at BC to earn his master's degree in secondary education. He also served as the graduated assistant and head assistant coach for the basketball team during those years.

The '84-'85 campaign was Mitch's seventh on the Massimino coaching staff. Mitch had been promoted to assistant head coach in '82-'83, the title he carried through the championship season.

Marty Marbach

Marty graduated St. Francis of Loretto in 1975. He served as assistant head coach at Westfield State College in Massachusetts. The '84-'85 season was Marty's sixth on the Massimino staff. He began the stint as an intern assistant. The championship season was his first with the title of full-time assistant. Marty succeeded Paul Cormier at the post when Paul left for the head coaching job at Dartmouth College in the summer of 1984.

Steve Lappas

Steve was the newest addition to Rollie's coaching staff in the '84-'85 championship season. He came on board as a part-time assistant coach, replacing the slot vacated when Marty Marbach took over for the departed Paul Cormier. Steve graduated in 1977 from the City College of New York with a degree in elementary education. He played for CCNY for four years and was team captain as a senior, Steve had spent the previous five years as the head coach at Harry S. Truman High School in the Bronx. In the '83-'84 season, Steve's Truman Mustangs fashioned a 27-3 log and went on to take the New York City championship and New York State Class A Championship. As a high school coach, Steve was twice honored as Coach of the Year by the *New York Daily News*.

Steve was part of Coach Mass's staff through 1998 when he accepted the head coaching job at Manhattan College. In four years, he turned the program around. The Jaspers had won only 75 games in the eight years prior to his arrival. By his fourth and final season at Manhattan, Coach Lappas led his team to a 25-9 record, the best in school history. The NABC (National

Steve Lappas went on to coach the Wildcats after Rollie Massimino. (Photo courtesy of the Villanova Sports Information Department)

Association of Basketball Coaches) named Steve the District 2 Coach of the Year.

Steve was named head coach of Villanova in April 1992, replacing Rollie Massimino. Steve coached the Wildcats for the next nine seasons, compiling a 174-110 record, .613. Steve left Villanova in 2001, and took the head coaching job at University of Massachusetts.

Harry Booth

Harry was an experienced coach. He had graduated St. Joe's in 1962 with a BS degree in business management and immediately accepted the head coaching job at Bishop McDevitt after graduation. Next Harry served as St. Joe's assistant basketball coach from '66-'74. He was the head baseball coach for the Hawks from '74-'78. All in all, going into that championship season, Harry had coached four years in high school and twelve years in college. The '84-'85 campaign marked Harry's fourth season as volunteer assistant coach.

HARRY BOOTH: "I had gotten out of coaching. Honestly, I was really feeling down in the dumps, like I never wanted to coach again. For so many years, I had put St. Joe's ahead of everything. I didn't know if I could do that again. Rollie asked me if I'd consider being a volunteer coach. My wife said, 'You don't even like Rollie, and after all those years you spent at St. Joe's … St. Joe's and Villanova don't like each other too much in basketball! How's that going to work?' I had mixed emotions. Then I kind of slinked into the Field House on October 18 when the team was practicing, Ed Pinckney's freshman year. Next thing I know, John Pinone, Eddie, Dwayne, Mike Mulquin and others were walking over to me to try to convince me to coach. I was impressed at what nice kids they were. I gave it a week, then a month, then three months, and so on for several years. I grew to think the world of Rollie, and to respect him tremendously."

Harry had to juggle coaching and job commitments the whole time he was with Rollie. "When I couldn't make it to practice, Rollie inisted I come over to his house that night. I did, and we'd talk and talk strategy. His wife would make me

'spags'—delicious spags! Then I'd go home and my wife would have dinner for me. It was busy, but they were wonderful times."

APPENDIX

Rollie Massimino's Career

1956 Rollie is an assistant coach at Cranford (New Jersey) High School.

1959 Massimino gets his first head coaching job at Hillside (New Jersey) High School, his prep alma mater.

1963 He moves to Lexington (Massachusetts) High School and his squad cops a state championship. In 10 seasons as a high school coach, Massimino compiles a 160-61 record.

1969-70 Rollie is head coach at Stony Brook. The team goes 18-6 season with a perfect 8-0 in its conference to take the title. Team loses to Buffalo State 93-69 in the first round of the NCAA.

1970-71 Rollie ends his stint at Stony Brook with a 15-10 mark and second-place finish in conference play.

1971-72 Massimino is hired by future NBA and U.S. Olympic head coach Chuck Daly as an assistant coach at Penn. The 25-3 Quakers reach the Sweet 16 of the NCAA Tournament and capture the Ivy League title (13-1 mark).

1972-73 Penn again reaches the Sweet 16 of the NCAA Tournament. The Quakers again take the Ivy League championship, with a 12-2 record, and finish 21-7 overall.

1973-74 Massimino is named head coach at Villanova on November 13, 1973. His team goes 7-19 in his first year.

1975-76 Massimino records his first winning season at Villanova with a 16-11 campaign. The team reaches the ECAC playoffs and is co-champions of Philadelphia's Big 5.

1976-77 Massimino gets his first-ever postseason NIT bid at Villanova.

1977-78 Massimino's 23-9 Wildcats earn their first NCAA Division I Tournament bid in the Massimino era (following a six-year hiatus). 'Nova downs Indiana before losing to Duke.

1979-80 Frosh John Pinone leads the 23-8 'Cats to an NCAA bid. Rollie records his 100th win with a 93-66 win over St. Francis (PA) on December 28, 1979.

1980-81 Massimino captures the Sun Bowl Tournament en route to a 20-11 campaign, a Big East Tournament runner-up and NCAA bid. 'Nova downs the Houston Cougars before losing to Virginia.

1981-82 The Wildcats capture the Big East Title outright with an 11-3 mark and a 24-8 overall slate. They lose in the Big East

Tournament title game, and reach the NCAA Elite Eight with triumphs over Northeastern and Memphis State.

1982-83 The Wildcats post their second consecutive 24-8 campaigns and first-place honors in the Big East. The team advances to the NCAA Elite Eight.

1983-84 The Wildcats earned their second consecutive tie for the Big East regular season crown with a 12-4 conference mark. In the NCAA Tournament, 'Nova downs Marshall in the first round before losing to Illinois.

1984-85 'Nova wins its only national championship. Massimino is honored as National Coach of the Year. Ed Pinckney wins NCAA Tournament MVP. The 25 wins are a single-season best for Coach Massimino.

1985-86 Massimino's squad wins 23, including 10 victories and a third place in the Big East. 'Nova upends Virginia Tech in the NCAA's before losing to Georgia Tech.

1987-88 The 24-13 'Cats match the school record for most games played in a season. They advance to the NCAA Elite Eight for the fifth time in 11 years. Oklahoma defeats the 'Cats to halt their march.

1988-89 Rollie records his 300th NCAA Division I win with a 76-67 win over Providence on January 4, 1989.

1991-92 In his final year at Villanova, Massimino and his squad go to the NIT and finish fourth in the tough Big East. The NIT was Massimino's 13th straight postseason tournament appearance and 15th overall in his 19 years at 'Nova.

1992-93 Massimino accepts the head coaching job at UNLV. The Runnin' Rebels finish 21-8 and earn an NIT spot. Massimino records his tenth 20+ win campaign.

1993-94 In his second and final season at UNLV, Massimino's Runnin' Rebels go 15-13 and finish fifth in the Big West. The Rebs do not receive a postseason bid, shattering a 14-year run of postseason tournament action for Massimino.

1996-97 Massimino inks a four-year contract to become the 12th coach in the history of Cleveland State Men's Basketball. The Vikings post 9-19 overall and 6-10 (sixth place) MCC records.

1998-99 Massimino guides the Vikings to a 13-13 regular-season mark in his third season, the first time since 1992-93 (22-5) that CSU finishes at or above .500 during the regular season. Massimino picks up his 450th career victory against Prairie View A&M on December 19, 1998.

1999-2000 In Massimino's fourth season, the Vikings finish 16-14 for their first winning season since 1992-93. Massimino picks up his 50th victory at CSU with a win over Stony Brook on February 16.

2000-2001 The Cleveland State Vikings go 19-13. Despite an overall record of 35-48 under Massimino's helm at Cleveland State, Massimino signs a contract extension to keep him through the 2004-2005 season.

March 15, 2003 After a twenty-loss season, and after tallying a seven-year 90-113 log and troubling off-court issues, Cleveland State buys out the final two years of Massimino's contract. Massimino resigns.

Important Dates in Villanova Sports History

May 2, 1866 Villanova's first varsity team takes the field for an auspicious debut. Villanova scores a 74-9 victory over the Central Club of Philadelphia in baseball.

April 30, 1870 Villanova plays its first intercollegiate game, besting Haverford College 66-21.

November 22, 1894 Villanova plays and wins its first football game against Logan AA, 24-0.

December 21, 1920 The men's basketball team records a 43-40 win over Catholic University in its first ever NCAA men's basketball game.

April 25, 1925 Villanova ran its first race in the Penn Relays.

May 2, 1925 Villanova holds its first dual track meet against Temple.

1926 The name "Wildcats" replaces "Blue & White" as the team name.

1929 Jake Nevin becomes a Villanova trainer under Harry Stuhldreher, football coach (and one of Notre Dame's "Four Horsemen").

March 5, 1932 Temple spoils the dedication of the new Villanova Field House by defeating the 'Cats, in basketball, 29-25.

1936 In his Villanova coaching debut, legendary basketball coach Al Severance upends Seton Hall 25-21, the first of his 413 career wins.

March 16, 1939 The basketball team had ousted Brown University to move into the first-ever NCAA Final Four, but eventual tournament champion Ohio State topples the Wildcats 53-26.

March 11, 1961 Al Severance loses 82-80 to Penn at the Palestra to close out an illustrious 25-year Villanova coaching career with a 413-201 mark.

December 2, 1961 Jack Kraft kicks off his Villanova coaching career with an 81-64 drubbing of Scranton.

January, 1966 The men's basketball team plays its 1,000th game, marking the occasion with a 62-48 pasting of St. Peter's at the Field House.

March 27, 1971 The men's basketball team celebrates Villanova's 50th year of hardwood competition by coming oh-so-close to upsetting the unsinkable UCLA juggernaut of the John Wooden era. Jack Kraft receives the "NCAA Coach of the Year" award.

December 1, 1973 Roland V. Massimino launches his legendary Villanova coaching career with a 71-58 spanking of Richmond.

November 28, 1978 Harry Perretta coaches his first game as pilot of the woman's basketball team, crushing Philadelphia Textile (now Philadelphia College) 65-38.

March 13, 1980 Villanova announces they will join the Big East Conference.

September 27, 1980 Villanova Stadium reopens with Astroturf, lights, and a new track. During the halftime dedication ceremonies, the track is dedicated to "Jumbo" Jim Elliott whose former runners, including Villanova's 32 Olympians (at that time), return to honor him. Fittingly, the Wildcats score an impressive 20-9 win over the Eagles of Boston College.

March 22, 1981 Jumbo Jim Elliott dies of a heart attack. He coached Villanova track for 45 years.

April 14, 1981 After suffering financial losses due to poor attendance, the Villanova Division I football program is scrapped.

March 26, 1982 Harry Perretta's woman's basketball team mirror-images the men's team's feat of 1939. In the last-ever AIWA National Championship Tournament, the 'Cats fall 83-75 to Rutgers in the semi-finals (the '39 men's team lost in the same round to Brown in the first-ever NCAA Tournament). The woman's team finished third in the tournament and fashioned a 29-4 seasonal record.

December 13, 1983 The board of trustees for the university announces plans to reinstate football at the Division I-AA level.

February 27, 1985 The Villanova Field House, for years referred to (with apprehension, by opponents) as the "'Cat House," is renamed "The Jake Nevin Field House."

April 1, 1985 Alexander G. Severance dies of a massive coronary in Lexington Kentucky on the morning of Villanova basketball's crowning achievement—winning the 1985 NCAA Tournament.

September 5, 1985 Villanova reinstitutes football under new coach Andy Talley. The 'Cats start with a bang—a 27-7 shellacking of Iona, and go on to an undefeated, 5-0-0 season.

December 9, 1985 John "Jake" Nevin dies at 75 of Lou Gehrig's Disease. He was a trainer at Villanova for 56 years.

January 4, 1986 The defending national champion Villanova Wildcats play their final game in the Jake Nevin Field House, their home court for the preceding 32 years. The farewell featured an 87-71 trouncing of Marist. The Field House was voted by *Inside Sports* as one of the ten places college coaches most hate to visit—a (left-handed) compliment to Wildcat fans as much as the guys out there in shorts.

January 22, 1986 The Wildcat women basketballers beat the men's team to the punch. Two weeks prior to the official opening of the new John E. duPont Pavilion, the women outscore Pittsburgh 62-53.

February 1, 1986 Now the duPont Pavilion officially opens. The men christen the facility with a 64-62 squeaker over Maryland televised on NBC.

March 30, 1987 Shelly Pennefather wins the Margaret Wade Trophy as the national woman's basketball Player of the Year. Shelly tops the all-time list of Villanova hardwood scorers—men and women—with 2,408 points. She led the 'Cats to back-to-back Big East Championships.

Wildcat baseball, football, and basketball (men and women) teams all won their debuts. The football team did it twice— once in 1894 and again in 1985 as a Division I-AA competitor. The basketball team christened and closed the Villanova (Jake Nevin) Field House with victories, before debuting with a win at the duPont Pavilion. The women won their first ever basketball game, and won their debut at the duPont Pavilion. Wildcat athletes have shown a penchant for making a big moment momentous.

EPILOGUE

"Checkered" might best describe Villanova University's post-1985 history, both on and off the hardwood. Sadly, the championship euphoria took a jolt not long after the victory when an article authored by Villanova's own Gary McLain appeared in the March 16, 1987 issue of *Sports Illustrated*. McLain, whose ball-handling was so instrumental in the Villanova victory over Georgetown, penned a 17-page exposé that painted an unflattering, if not seamy, portrayal of his Villanova experience. Early on in his reportage, McLain recounted the '85 championship squad's congratulatory visit to the White House: "President Reagan was welcoming my teammates and me at the White House and giving his little speech about how inspirational our victory was ... And the cocaine had me floating in my own private world." In his jaw-dropping account, the former 'Nova guard went on to say he was: "Thinking thoughts like, *I could push him [Reagan] in the head, just a little tap, and make news all over the world.* That's how high I was."

McLain's story rocked his teammates, his alma mater, and the NCAA. McLain related that he had confronted Coach Rollie Massimino various times about drug use. In McLain's version, Massimino had told him: "I hear you're on cocaine, or selling it. If I find out, you're gone." McLain added that Massimino never pressed the issue. Nor were urinalysis tests ever ordered. For a coach who had carefully cultivated an image that character-building nurtured by paternal love and discipline was the pillar of his program, the assertions must have been devastating.

McLain's article cast a wide net. He impugned not only Massimino, but also Rev. John P. Stack, OSA, Dean of Students, and his teammates as being aware of McLain's alleged illegalities and, as McLain implied, turning a blind eye. McClain even roped alumni into the intrigue, charging that one unnamed alumnus lent him money. McLain related that he would, "borrow a few dollars from some alums. Not high-powered types. Just some guys I knew. Borrow, that is, while knowing it wasn't really 'borrow,' but, 'Pay it back whenever.'" McLain didn't name the alumni nor specify that the alumni knew how the money was being used. Still, consistent with the tenor of the overall article, the assertion was unsettling.

Unfortunately, this episode wasn't Villanova's first NCAA blemish. In 1971, Villanova became the first team that ever played in the NCAA Tournament finals and had their results stricken from the NCAA record books due to a rules violation (since that year, three other teams have suffered the same humiliation). The NCAA took the action because the 'Cats' Howard Porter had signed a professional contract with the Pittsburgh Condors of the American Basketball Association in the middle of his senior year thus making him ineligible for the Tournament.

The NCAA action stung, especially since it eradicated Porter's selection as the 1971 NCAA Tournament's Most Outstanding Player. It was even more unfortunate because

Villanova, arguably, had given UCLA the most, and perhaps only, competitive contest in the Bruins' unprecedented run of seven straight NCAA championships [and ten of twelve NCAA championships from 1967 to 1975], at least in terms of the championship game itself. Prior to Villanova, no UCLA championship-game opponent came within 11 points of the Bruins. Villanova lost a hard-fought 68-62 battle to the high-powered Sidney Wicks- and Curtis Rowe-led Bruins.

From 1985 till the Wright Era

The Wildcats have competed in the NCAA Tournament 17 times since 1985. Only 12 times did the 'Cats miss out. In nine of those 12 NCAA-Tournament-deprived postseasons, Villanova still played in the NIT. And, in 1994, the Wildcats copped an NIT Tournament title.

That's certainly not a shabby record, although I suspect that some, if not most Villanovans, had set the post-'85 expectations-bar higher. The year after the '85 championship, the Wildcats' 23-14 record was only 3 games off the champions' 25-10 log. But the departure of the seasoned Pinckney-McLain-McClain triumvirate proved too big a loss. The 1986 'Cats made it only as far as the second round of the NCAA before succumbing to Georgia Tech. The following season, Villanova slumped to 14-15, registering their first losing season since 1975 [a year that marked the end of a streak of three consecutive losing campaigns.]

Villanova regained its mojo again in 1988 when the Main Liners clawed past Arkansas, Illinois, and Kentucky in succession. The victories propelled them into the Elite 8. The ride ended there. Oklahoma dismantled the 'Cats 78-59 in the Southeast Regional Finals in Birmingham, Alabama, depriving them of a trip to the Final Four. It would take more than two decades for Villanova to advance that far again.

The last year that a Rollie Massimino-coached Villanova team competed in the NCAA Tournament was 1989. Disappointingly, the 'Cats fell in the first round to LSU. Two years later, after a 14-15 campaign in 1991-92, Rollie Massimino left Villanova.

In fact, 1989 turned out to be the last time any Rollie Massimino-coached team would compete in the NCAA Tournament. Rollie left 'Nova to accept the head coaching job at the University of Nevada Las Vegas. The hope that he would restore credibility—and success—to the beleaguered UNLV program went unfulfilled. When Massimino arrived at UNLV, the basketball team was on probation. Its long-time, high-profile coach Jerry Tarkanian had been forced to resign under suspicion of various infractions. Rollie left UNLV only two years later, after it came out that Massimino and UNLV president Robert Maxson had cut a side deal that lifted Massimino's salary well beyond the figure reported to the state of Nevada.

Massimino's woes didn't end. He moved on to Cleveland State. Hired with the expectation he'd lift a woeful program into respectability, Rollie called it quits after an 8-22 season and a dead-last finish in the nine-team Horizon League. Off-court problems persisted. Two of his former Cleveland State charges, Damon Stringer and Jamaal Harris, were convicted of robbing [then] Cleveland Indians pitcher C.C. Sabathia at gunpoint in a downtown hotel. Stringer and Harris both received four-year sentences. Prior to Massimino's final season, two of his players transferred, and later Massimino dismissed leading scorer Modibo Niakate for unspecified disciplinary reasons.

His years at Cleveland State behind him, Rollie Massimino ended up at Northwood University in West Palm Beach, Florida, where he has been head coach since 2006.

After Massimino's departure from Villanova, Steve Lappas took over the head coaching job at Villanova. His debut season was dismal. The 'Cats went 8-19 with a worst-ever 3-15 record on the Big East slate. Redemption came the following season when Lappas took the 20-12 'Cats to Villanova's first and only NIT championship.

The Lappas era lasted three more seasons. In only one of them did Villanova receive a bid to the NCAA tournament, and in that one appearance, Villanova suffered a first-game elimination.

In the midst of the Lappas era, the University endured yet another embarrassing episode. In 1985, Villanova replaced its original basketball venue, the Villanova Field House, which had been built in 1932 and later redubbed the Jake Nevin Field House [you can read some Jake stories elsewhere in this book]. The new structure with its striking hyperbolic paraboloid roofline was originally known as John Eleuthère du Pont Pavilion, in honor of its funder, John Eleuthère du Pont—he of the wealthy, influential du Pont family. However in 1997, the du Pont name was removed from the facility, apparently with the family's tacit permission, after John was convicted of murdering Olympic wrestling gold medalist Dave Schultz. The disturbing story is the subject of the 2014 film *Foxcatcher*, with an all-star cast of Steve Carrell, Mark Ruffalo, Channing Tatum, Vanessa Redgrave, and Sienna Miller (and currently rated a superb 88 percent/98 percent on *Rotten Tomatoes*).

The Wright Era

Jay Wright succeeded Lappas for the 2000-2001 season, and debuted with a 19-13 record. Then the sophomore jinx struck, and Villanova posted a losing record—one of only two in the continuing Wright era. By 2005, Villanova made it to the Sweet 16 once more—its most successful NCAA Tournament performance since 1988. With stars like Philadelphia's Randy Foye [of Cardinal Dougherty HS], Allan Ray, and Curtis

Sumpter leading the way, Villanova soared to a 24-8 record.

In the Syracuse semifinals, the Wildcats lost a 67-66 heartbreaker to North Carolina. Villanova dropped behind 64-54 with 3:45 left in the contest, but deftly cut the deficit to 66-63. With only a few ticks left on the clock, Villanova's Allan Ray drove the lane and shot. As he made the basket, there was contact. The Villanova faithful jumped to their feet, but quickly sat back down. Ray was called for traveling. Replays seemed to substantiate that Ray had not traveled. But the call stuck and North Carolina held on for a controversial victory.

The following season, 2006, the 'Cats earned their first-ever No. 1 NCAA Tournament seed. In the Regional Semifinals, they matched up against Boston College. Actually, it was more like *mismatched*. Only one Villanova starter was taller than 6'4" while *every* BC starter topped 6'4". The game was nip and tuck all the way. In a tense overtime period, with the Wildcats down by one and the clock ticking down to its last tick, 6'8" Will Sheridan of Villanova flipped a layup skyward. BC's Sean Williams went up and swiped it away—above the rim. The referee ruled goaltending and Villanova celebrated a one-point win. Villanova couldn't advance after that though. Florida slammed the door to Villanova's national championship dreams in the Regional Finals with a resounding 75-62 win over the 'Cats.

Again in 2008, Wright's squad charged to the Regional semifinals, only to get dumped 72-57 by Kansas. But good things were on the horizon.

In 2009, Villanova was seeded No. 3 in the East Regional at Boston. The 'Cats dispatched American, UCLA, and Duke easily in the first three rounds. The lowest victory margin in any game was 13 points. Then in a tense Regional Final against No. 1 Pittsburgh, Scottie Reynolds's ¾-court dash culminated in a buzzer-beating jump shot to give 'Nova an exciting two-point, 78-76 victory over the Panthers. Reynolds who was voted Most Outstanding Player in the East Regional Tourney, joined fellow

'Cats Dwayne Anderson and Dante Cunningham on the All-East Regional Tournament team.

Villanova had advanced to the Final Four. Unfortunately, North Carolina stymied the Wildcats from reaching the championship game. North Carolina's early run of 11 unanswered points proved too much, and the Tar Heels prevailed 83-69.

In 2011, Villanova University was once again rocked by scandal. This time it was the Villanova Law School, which disclosed early that year that it had falsified admissions data for incoming freshmen for an unknown period prior to 2010. The school posted an embarrassing message on its website: "Because the misconduct was intentional and long-standing and because it is so fundamentally inconsistent with basic concepts underlying AALS' [American Association of Law Schools] core values and bylaws, the executive committee condemns these actions and places the law school on probation for a period of two years."

The Law School imbroglio mirrored some of the hard-court woes of the 2010 NCAA Tournament. After a successful 25-8/13-5 regular season, the Main Liners, ranked No. 9 in the AP, were rewarded with a No. 2 seed in the South Regional bracket. The Tournament started badly and bizarrely. Incredibly, Villanova needed an overtime period to subdue unsung Robert Morris, 73-70. The game was strange from the get-go. To make what he called "a teaching point," Coach Wright kept Scottie Reynolds out of the starting lineup. Reynolds nonetheless went on to tally 20 points, but, uncharacteristically, did so while making only 2 of 15 shots from the field.

Rather than shake off the first-round shock, Villanova and star guard Scottie Reynolds remained in a funk. In Villanova's second—and what proved to be final—game, St. Mary's' Omar Samhan scored 32 points and grabbed seven rebounds as the No. 10 St. Mary's shocked 'Nova, 75–68 and sent the 'Cats home. Reynolds scored only 8 points in the contest.

In the three most recent seasons (2012-14), Villanova has made the NCAA Tournament twice but failed to break through to the second round. Still, given Villanova's track record, it's likely a matter of time before another national contender comes along.

A Look Back

The David and Goliath portrayal of the 1985 NCAA champions as written and entered in sports lore belongs to the ages. There's no tweaking the narrative.

That's why an hour of my interview with ESPN a few years ago landed on the cutting-room floor. ESPN was doing a piece about the '85 Wildcats' "miracle" victory over Georgetown. Unfortunately, I didn't feed into the "Which- 'Wonder of the World' -should-we-assign-this-game?" fervor that fueled the documentary.

I've come to attribute the Villanova victory to math. Yes, as unsexy as that might sound. Math, as in statistics—the mathematical science that, among other things, predicts the relative probability of outcomes—tells me the answer. So pervasive is the use of statistics that you'd be hard-pressed to identify anything in your daily life *not* touched by statistical analysis. You know, if a machine produces widgets, how many widgets have to be tested, and at what intervals, in order for the producer to be 90 percent certain the machine isn't turning out defective widgets? The marketplace brims with widgets. Everything you own, buy, and see is subjected to the rigors of statistics.

If we consider the outcome of the Villanova-Georgetown game statistically, was a Villanova victory the probable outcome? No. Was it an impossible outcome? No. Was it a plausible outcome? Yes. The outcome was not *the* most probable, but, unarguably, it was possible.

The anecdotal representation of that reasoning appears in Ed Pinckney's analysis of the game: "Georgetown was good, but they weren't out of our league. If we played Georgetown ten times, I think we would have beaten them three or four times. It's not like we were totally outclassed. After all, we knew these guys. We knew them for a long time. It's not like we came from some other part of the country and never competed. Several guys on our team had played against several of their guys in various leagues from grade school through high school and college. We weren't afraid or intimidated by their reputation. And we sure didn't walk out on the court that night expecting to lose. We expected to win."

Endlessly analyzing every facet of the game makes entertaining conversation fueling today's 24-hour sports cycle with repartee that is too often humorously full of sound and fury that signifies nothing. Logically, the search for the one, esoteric, cryptic "open sesame" reason that unlocks the mystery and supplies the "why" for one improbable, but not implausible, basketball victory is moot.

Contrivances like "Villa-nowhere" augment the wonderment that shrouds the game. But it's a contrivance. Villa-nowhere is laughably wrong. Villanova appeared in the inaugural, 1939, NCAA Tournament. Villanova has appeared in four Final Four matchups. Villanova has appeared more times in the NCAA Tournament than all but seven other teams in the entire nation. Villanova's all-time winning percentage also ranks No. 20 among all Division I programs. Villanova is not "nowhere." It's somewhere, and that somewhere is generally wherever the NCAA Tournament is taking place.

Yes, the Villanova victory was unquestionably an upset. But as upsets go, it certainly pales to, let's say, No. 15 Lehigh University's toppling of No. 2 Duke in the 2012 NCAA Tournament. You see, in boxing terms, the '85 Villanova squad had a puncher's chance. They had a team full of guys on basketball scholarships with a searing focus on playing basketball as a career. A few of them were headed to the NBA. They were quite capable of landing a punch—even a lucky punch—and defeating Georgetown. Lehigh, with no scholarships and virtually no history in the NCAA Tournament, had nothing remotely resembling a puncher's chance. Yet they won. Why? How? For the same reason that Villanova won. Math. If Lehigh played Duke 1,000 times, they'd beat them *once*. That "once" came on March 16, 2012.

Villanova had such a night in the '85 Finals. In Villanova's case, they met Georgetown on one of the three or four nights out of ten that Villanova would have—could have—won. Naturally, there were important factors that contributed to the upset. Villanova's slow pace jostled Georgetown out of its comfort zone, and knocked them off their rhythm. But a slow-down strategy against a superior opponent is not earth-shattering. Several teams over the years have employed the technique with success. But the strategy was far from unique. Nor should it have been unexpected, as contrasted with, let's say, Muhammed Ali's genius in concocting, on the spot, his brilliant, never-before-seen, rope-a-dope strategy to "upset" the considered-invincible George Foreman. Villanova shot the ball spectacularly well, and Gary McLain thwarted Georgetown's vaunted defensive pressure. And of the three or four games out of ten that Villanova would win if the two teams played ten times, the April 1, 1985 match turned out to be Villanova's night. That doesn't diminish the achievement nor destroy the entertaining account of a team that over-achieved that's told in these pages. So, hats off to the Wildcats for shining when it counted.

—Robert Gordon, Summer 2014